The Greatest
GIFT
A Return to Hope

Kathy,
w/ great hope!
John O'Shaughnessy

JOHN O'SHAUGHNESSY

FERNE PRESS

Summary: A family deals with a wife and mother's terminal disease and learns many lessons along the way.

Library of Congress Cataloging-in-Publication Data
O'Shaughnessy, John
The Greatest Gift: A Return to Hope / John O'Shaughnessy –
First Edition
ISBN: 978-1-933916-08-8
1. Grief 2. Loss 3. Bereavement 4. Death 5. Widowers 6. Terminal disease
I. O'Shaughnessy, John   II. Title
Library of Congress Control Number: 2007926659

Design concepts by Eric O'Shaughnessy

FERNE PRESS

Ferne Press is an imprint of Nelson Publishing & Marketing
366 Welch Road, Northville, MI 48167
www.nelsonpublishingandmarketing.com
(248) 735-0418

This book is based on my life with Ann Catherine O'Shaughnessy, my wife. From beginning to end, the story line is true. At times, when needed, my imagination blended with my recollection to complete an event or thought. If you read this story with an open mind, it's all real.

ACKNOWLEDGMENTS

I would like to acknowledge all the people who helped create this story. For making countless trips through Canada to lend a loving, helping hand to their daughter, son-in-law, and grandsons in Michigan, I wish to thank Ann's mother and father, Joyce and Arnie Swable. Without them, none of this would have been possible. To my sons, Eric and Collin, who oftentimes blurred the lines between student and teacher. In both of them, I saw a bright light that allowed me to find my way home. Thanks to my family for their love and support. Thank you to Brian O'Shaughnessy for guiding me along this path. Thanks to Laureen Goguen for being the best friend Ann ever had. To Kathy Cross, Mary Lou Boyer, and Debbie Jahner, thanks for the long-distance nursing care they provided Ann. Special thanks to all of our Michigan friends, especially Sharon Rittenhouse, Mary Mitsch, Mary Calabrese, and Ann Drake. When the winds blew and the rains came, we found shelter in their kindness, compassion, and most of all, their love. To my publisher, Marian Nelson, and my editor, Julayne Hughes, thank you for stretching this novice writer and helping me carve out something others could learn from.

Mostly, my thanks to Ann. I hope in the pages that follow I have accurately portrayed her courage, her spirit, and her love for all the people who were blessed to have known her and called her a friend, a daughter, a mother, and a wife. Ann was uniquely gifted in knowing what mattered most in life and it is with that thought that this story begins.

*A portion of the proceeds benefits the New Hope Center
for Grief Support, Northville, Michigan*

*Ann, you are thought of every day and remembered in the
countless ways you touched our hearts. We miss you.
Love Eric, Collin, and John*

In an instant, a split second in between heartbeats, life can change forever. This is the moment of impact when the pain is profound and felt in every cell of your body. You take long, deep breaths as your world spins out of control on some unknown axis.

1 | We Were Blessed

*Everything happens for a reason and sometimes we don't get to
know what that reason is until someone else decides to tell us.*

The last few weeks of Ann's life took place in our dining room, by a large bay window that overlooked the back yard where every morning she woke to the sound of birds singing. She loved this room. She loved the warmth and light from the afternoon sun. She loved the wallpaper she chose and hung, for it was bright and cheery with flowers of green and pink, her favorite colors. She loved the laughter that once echoed from this room. She loved helping her children with their homework and the meals she served here on special days for special people.

Sadly, as her life was nearing its end, this room was transformed from a dining room to a dying room. Her once-strong legs had atrophied and walking had become more difficult. She last slept upstairs when the weather was much warmer and the leaves much greener. She could no longer do the things she loved, like walk her boys to the bus stop, make her favorite meal, or retrieve the afternoon mail. She had no privacy and in many ways she was like a baby again. Those close to Ann knew death was near. Ann knew this as well and so the room was arranged to be her haven. Pictures of her handsome sons graced the shelf that overlooked their mother and on good days she looked at those pictures and saw grown men in the faces of the boys in the photos. The large oak dining table was pushed to one side to make room for the hospital bed where she slept. Chairs gathered around her where people leaned in close to her, holding her hand, not missing a word she said. Her breathing was assisted by an oxygen tank and a morphine pump eased her pain. Books were close by; cards, letters, a rosary, and a crucifix completed the room.

Friends came to visit her from thousands of miles away, just up the street, and many places in between. They came because they loved her. Some friends from places far away had said their goodbyes months before, not knowing if they would make it back in time before her last breath. Ann knew they wouldn't, and it was a painful separation. Closure for some would come in the form of a phone call letting them know that she slipped away peacefully in her dining room; friends and family were gathered around her when she died. She loved you very much. She is gone now.

We always left with a little more wisdom than when we came: wisdom from a dying woman who knew more about living than any of us did.

How appropriate, I thought, the dining room. For many years, Ann was the centerpiece of my life, her children's lives, and those of many others. After spending time with Ann in this room, we always seemed to leave better people. Sometimes we even left with smiles on our faces and when we did, she smiled too. We always left with a little more wisdom than when we came: wisdom from a dying woman who knew more about living than any of us did. I marveled at how Ann made us feel better in those final weeks of her life. It's one of the things that made her so special.

I'm not sure Ann ever understood why people kept coming to see her, but she was grateful they did. She loved it when someone held her hands, looked deep into her eyes, and told her how much they loved her. She appreciated all the cards and letters addressed to her that kept pouring in from far and near. She was thankful for the little things that most people took for granted, like a conversation with an old friend over a warm cup of tea.

At the end of her life, Ann gave back all she had left to give and took nothing with her but the love she had for us in her heart. She told me on one of those final days that she felt "blessed to have loved and been loved by so many wonderful people."

We were blessed too.

2 | Driftwood

*I had felt like driftwood, aimlessly going
wherever the currents moved me.*

I looked in on Ann as I did many times during those final days. She slept in a slightly upright position in the hospital bed brought by the hospice people. She hadn't moved in days. Her mouth remained in an open position taking in as much oxygen as her weakened body would allow. Soft shallow breaths she made. She was there, but she wasn't there, not the Ann I knew anyway. The heat was on inside this house, but if you peered in through her broken glass, you only saw one small light flickering in her interminable darkness.

I knew she wasn't sleeping but I preferred to call it that. It somehow made what she was going through easier for me and sounded more peaceful and less final than "coma." The hospice nurse had confirmed my suspicions that Ann would never wake again, that this was it and I was relieved I had said goodbye a few days before when she was still lucid.

And as I gazed at her, I reflected back to that magical night when we first met. The night she found me and we became one.

In early autumn of 1981, the weather had cooled and the leaves in New England had just begun to turn colors. On the tops of trees, yellow and orange leaves mixed in with the green ones and though it was not as breathtaking as it would be in the middle of October when the foliage was at its peak, it was something to look forward to. Even though summer was over, New Englanders like me loved this time of year for the air was crisp and dry, and if only for a short while, the landscape was painted with such splendor.

I had graduated two years earlier earning my bachelor's degree in business management from the University of Lowell, a state university known for the education of future engineers and teachers. I was neither. I sold food and sundries to grocery stores: tuna fish, raisins, candy, even light bulbs. The list was long. It was

The lights in my life were always yellow, which meant I never had to stop and think.

a respectable way to make a living, but hardly that impressive. My world at my young age was coming and going. The lights in my life were always yellow, which meant I never had to stop and think. I kept running through the intersections looking straight ahead. Problem was, I was on the wrong road; I needed a red light to stop me in my tracks.

I dated. My first love and I had broken up a few months back. I wasn't over her but dated anyway. I told my mother I knew one thing, I would never find my future wife in a bar.

The Dubliner was a smoked-filled Irish tavern in Lowell, Massachusetts. Lowell was known at the turn of the century as a textile town and the Dubliner was an old factory where I think they made sweaters, socks, or perhaps undergarments. It had wide-planked wooden floors that were scuffed up from all the foot traffic and brick walls decorated with pictures of weathered Irish faces, maps of Ireland, and green four-leaf clovers. Irish bands came to play sing-along music and the more people drank the more they sang along. By the end of the night sometimes the band could barely be heard at all.

It was time for me, I thought, to take a break from dating, from girls, to hang with the guys, to play some basketball at the YMCA, drink beer, and sing Irish songs. That was my plan that night I walked into the Dubliner, until I met Ann.

I would learn later that Ann noticed me the moment she walked in. She liked the preppy type and that was me. I'd guess it was the green cotton polo shirt and blue jeans that caught her eye that night. I never noticed her, but I wasn't looking, either.

The band had yet to begin playing and patrons were still piling in looking for good seats or any seats at all. In the corner of my eye I caught someone approaching my table.

"Hello. I'm Ann, and I wanted to thank you for the beer you sent to my table."

She smiled at me; her teeth glistened against her darkly tanned skin and she looked me dead in the eyes as if peering inside my soul to see if I was worth all this trouble she was going through.

"Hello, Ann," I replied. "I didn't buy you that beer, but if you like, I could buy you the next one."

"Then you wouldn't mind if my friend, Karen, and I joined you?"

"Not at all. My name is John." I held out my hand for her to shake, then she motioned for Karen who was just a few tables away to come join us.

"So what brings you here to Lowell?" I asked as I pulled the stools in closer to the table where we all gathered. I looked around for our waitress and waved to her. My friend, Carl, caught my eye and winked broadly at me. Now I knew where the beer had come from and perhaps I thought by the end of the night I would owe him a big favor.

"Karen convinced me it would be a fun thing to do. Go out on the town. Someplace we've never been before, have a few drinks and let our hair down. So here we are."

Karen and I exchanged greetings and it was then that I noticed the slight glaze over Ann's eyes that told me she had had a head start on the beer consumption. Perhaps that helped explain where she got the nerve to come talk to me.

"Are you from around here, John?"

"I'm from Chelmsford, but I live here in Lowell now."

"Never heard of Chelmsford, how do you say it?"

"CHELMS-Ford." I replied, with emphasis on the "Chelms."

"I'm from Buffalo, New York. Well, really the country outside Buffalo, in Darien, New York. It's about thirty miles east of Buffalo."

I paused for a moment and felt it rude not to introduce Ann and Karen to the rest of the table. Besides, I was hoping Karen might find someone else to talk with and leave Ann and me alone. It worked.

I turned my head toward my right shoulder and looked at Ann.

"So you're a nurse?"

"Yes, in Woburn, are you familiar with where that is?" Ann asked me as she sipped on her beer that had just arrived.

"I do. I'm in the grocery business. I sell food products to grocery stores. There's a store I go to in Woburn."

I wished fervently that I did something else. I wished I was a lawyer or a dentist, something impressive sounding, but I wasn't. I sold food and Ann didn't seem to mind. But I quickly tried to divert attention away from my profession.

"So Buffalo, you get a lot of snow there, don't you?"

"It's overrated. We have a big storm or two every year but it's not that bad. Weather here is just about the same."

"You must have family back there still?"

"Yes, my mom and dad, my sister, and two brothers still live there. I am the only one to move away so far, but I doubt anyone else will. I miss them but I needed to go to a bigger city and I always liked Boston, so here I am. I came here right after I finished nursing school."

As the night moved on, I was flirting as much with Ann as she was with me. She must have seen something in me I didn't see myself. In this dusky tavern on the high-topped stools on which we sat, we seemed to have an instant chemistry. By now, my back faced my friends and my eyes and attention were locked on this new woman with the pretty hazel eyes and thick shoulder-length auburn hair. She had this shyness about her that I was instantly attracted to and she'd often tilt her head a certain way when she smiled or laughed. Most importantly, I felt I didn't have to pretend to be someone I wasn't, like I was on an interview trying to impress my future boss. I liked that about her, unassuming and genuine.

When the band started playing, we raised our voices to a soft yell and spoke closer to each other. Often, when the singing was too loud, Ann spoke directly into my ear and there was something sensual with every wisp of breath I felt with each spoken word. We talked for hours that night, we sang along to the songs we knew and even the ones we didn't:

"Finnegan's Wake," "Whiskey in the Jar," and "Oh, Danny Boy." The night went quickly. Before we knew it, the band had stopped playing and it was time to go home.

"Well, John, it was nice to meet you. Can I give you my phone number? I will only give it to you if you promise to call me and I don't want you to think I give it out to everyone I meet, just the ones I like. By the way, my last name is Swable."

"I would love to take your number. When is a good time to call you?"

Ann apparently didn't carry a purse, so she sent Karen fishing through her bag to find a writing instrument for her. Seeing what was going on, I reached for my wallet, pulled out a business card, and handed it to Ann. As she scribbled her number on the back of the card, I once again noticed her tanned skin. Her only piece of jewelry was a gold bracelet on her left wrist. She handed me back my card and then reached in closer to me giving me a hug. She whispered in my ear and in the quiet of the pub I heard her say, "Soon."

By the time we left there was a rolling mist of precipitation in the air. The sky was the color of still deep water and without the street lights it might have felt as if we were walking on the dark side of the moon. Ann went one way and I went another and with each step our backs grew further apart. After a few steps I turned and looked for her, but she had vanished into the night.

As I drove home I couldn't stop thinking about her. How our conversation was so natural and smooth as if we'd been the best of friends for years. Perhaps it was the alcohol, I thought, but I wanted to dismiss that notion as quickly as it entered my mind. She was so beautiful and intelligent and at her young age, seemed to already have a blueprint for her life. She was so unlike me in that way. I had felt like driftwood aimlessly going wherever the currents moved me, and then it dawned on me that maybe the water had taken me to Ann and she was the sandy beach I would wash ashore on.

My self-talk consumed me the whole way home. Even after tucking myself into bed I lay awake restless and staring into the blackness of my bedroom, wondering what Ann was thinking about and if her thoughts were the same as mine.

Hello Mom,

    All is well. I'm busy sewing projects now that fall is here. How I love to keep busy. Thursday I'm signing up for dance lessons—Jazz, so I can be a sophisticated lady. I think I'll really like them. The news is "JOHN." The little Irishman called. We're going out Saturday night for dinner somewhere in Boston. It's a surprise, I'm excited about it. He's someone new, so no one knows him, so I don't have to hear stories. I can judge for myself. So far he's smart. He called and asked me out, so now to see if he's the "pot of gold." Keep your fingers crossed. I'll take the night for what it is. I'll let you know.

    Love you, miss you,
    Ann

    P.S. I bought a crock pot. $10.97!

3 | THE GREEN LIGHT

Ann seemed to know exactly what she wanted, and
every minute we were together, I felt as if she were sizing
me up to see if she wanted me.

I found out later that Ann had waited anxiously by the phone in her apartment as soon as she woke. She had hoped I would call, but really didn't think I would. I must have given her the impression that I wasn't interested in any lasting relationship with her. I must have given her the impression that her phone number meant nothing to me and perhaps I'd thrown it away or put it in some forgotten pile somewhere. And that the inescapable conclusion of our relationship had already happened the night before.

She couldn't have been more wrong.

At about nine, I stumbled from bed still groggy from the night before and started the coffee going. For me nothing much happened until that first cup. From the window in the kitchen I saw the rain was coming down in sheets and by the size of the puddles it looked like it had been raining for some time. I looked down at the counter and next to the coffee pot was my business card with Ann's phone number. Without hesitation, I began dialing.

"Hi Ann, this is John. I hope this isn't too early to call."

"No, it isn't John, I've already had my first Diet Coke and was about to jump in the shower. How are you?"

"I'm great, A little sleepy maybe. I had fun last night. I trust you and Karen made it home okay?"

"Well, actually, we got a little turned around, but we made it eventually. We talked the whole way home. She had as much fun as I did."

"So what did you and Karen talk about the whole way home?"

"It was just girl talk, nothing more than that. Besides, I barely know you and I can't tell you all of my secrets."

Outside the sky had become more ominous and long lightning strikes cut through the clouds, followed by the strident noise of thunder a few seconds later. It was the kind of day I wished I could curl up close to someone I loved, barefoot on the floor in front of a warm fire.

I sipped on my first swig of coffee. "Well, maybe someday you could tell me more about your girl talk. Ann, I would like to take you out again. Are you up for that, maybe next Saturday night?"

"I'll need to check my busy social calendar . . . Mmmm, it seems I'm tied up Monday, Wednesday, Thursday, and Friday, but you're in luck John, I'm free on Saturday. What time?"

"The luck of the Irish I guess. How about seven?"

"Sounds good. How should I dress?"

"I'll call you later this week after I have firmed up the plans. I can get directions to your apartment then too. Hey, stay dry and I'll call you in a few days."

We said our goodbyes and hung up. While I drank my coffee, I drew the curtains away from the sliding door and peered outside. The raindrops were getting larger, almost like they were mixed in with some heavy snow. The apartment I had was hardly alluring or even cozy, but for me it offered some personal space and independence. After all, I was twenty-four years old and most people my age no longer lived at home. They moved out, moved away, and got on with their adult lives. I was trying to do that. This was my attempt to break free from the driftwood and chart my own course. My mother cried the day I moved out of her house. I moved all of twenty minutes away, but she cried anyway.

Later that week, I called Ann. I told her to dress nice but not formal and that the weather called for a chilly evening so she should plan to wear a sweater or a light jacket. I loved her reply back. "Won't you keep me warm, John?"

I drove anxiously but confidently to her apartment in my white Mazda 626 sports car. Despite the chill in the air I kept the moon roof open and let the breeze tousle my hair. Music played loudly and I thought I looked the part of a wealthy young man who was successful beyond his years. I had no idea what kind of man Ann was looking for, but something inside of me hoped she was looking for me.

Along the way, I passed homes guarded by chain-link fences, drug stores in need of facelifts, and car dealers in need of customers. Grass sprouted from the pavement in the sidewalks and it appeared to me as though the street sweeper had not been by in quite some time. I drove by the hospital where Ann worked, then took a quick right down the hill onto Sturgess Street, where I saw her home on the left. I pulled up to the curb, going back and forth a little before I parked, making sure the passenger door was not obstructed so Ann could easily get in.

The house was old. It was white with black shutters, and, judging by the chipped paint, needed a fresh coat. It had a large front porch that over-looked the street and I imagined the owners enjoyed many a night out there. The yard was small and the lawn was in need of a good clipping.

I knocked on the side door and quickly heard footsteps coming down-stairs to greet me and invite me in.

I followed her up a narrow staircase. The steps had no carpet and had started to take on the shape of footsteps. When we reached the top, I smiled at Ann and gently pulled her in closer to me.

"May I have a hug?"

"You may and you don't even have to ask."

She was stunning in a white miniskirt with a matching top, her skin bronzed from the countless hours she'd spent basking in the sun. She was all of five foot three and my chin rested comfortably on the top of her head when I hugged her.

The embrace was short but tender and gave me something to look forward to. She held my hand and we walked.

"Can I give you a quick tour? It's not much to look at really, but I can walk to work. That's the best part of this place. My landlord can be a little cranky at times, but it will do for now. All the rooms are small but he pays for the heat and the electric so I can keep it as warm or as cool as I like."

Her apartment was unassuming, just as I thought Ann was. Narrow wooden hallways squeaked with every step and led to four small rooms and a tiny bathroom. I peeked inside her bedroom and saw an unmade mattress on the floor and some clothes scattered on and near it. I imagined she had trouble deciding her outfit but I liked that she wasn't obsessed with neatness or making an impression she couldn't sustain.

Every minute I was with Ann, I learned more about who she was. She had a zest for life, but was measured in all her moves. She seemed to know exactly what she wanted, and every minute we were together, I felt as if she were sizing me up to see if she wanted me.

"Where are we going tonight, John?"

"I thought we'd go to Quincy Market, have some dinner, and walk around the marketplace. How does that sound?"

"John, I love downtown Boston, how did you know?"

"There's that Irish luck again."

I wore a lightweight sports coat and Ann grabbed a sweater for when the night would get colder. We went down the narrow staircase, out the door, and down the paved path along the side of the house to the curb in the street and a perfectly parked white sports car that drove like the wind.

I opened Ann's door and was careful not to catch her skirt when I closed it behind her.

"Nice car, it smells new," Ann remarked.

"Because it is, I've only had it for about five months. I like it. Kind of sporty, don't you think?"

"Yes, I agree, very cute."

Trying to find the quickest way back to the highway, I took a few wrong turns, but Ann was nice enough not to laugh and got us back on course. I wanted her to think I knew my way around Boston, but I didn't, as I had led a less exploratory life closer to home. I wanted her to think the sports car was paid for too, but it wasn't and never would be.

We headed south as we turned onto the major artery that connects Boston to the suburbs north. We passed by old four-tenement homes that seemed to be within an arm's reach of the highway and I wondered if the vociferous roar of transportation was something the tenants ever got used to. As we gained speed it was getting dark, but off in the distance, peeking from behind houses and buildings, we could see the skyline of Boston. It was home to the Red Sox, the Celtics, and the Bruins, and was the birthplace so much of our nation's history, but for tonight the only thing that mattered was that it was the home to my first date with Ann.

"Isn't it a pretty view, John, all the lights in all the tall buildings? Buffalo is not as pretty as this."

"It's sad for me to say this, but you may have spent more time down here than I have. But I have to agree with you, it is a pretty sight. As a young boy, I went to the tops of both the Prudential and Hancock buildings. I don't know how they build those things."

We passed Bunker Hill, a famous historic landmark where a battle took place many years ago. Ann said she'd been there. I hadn't. She asked if I'd ever seen the ship where the tea party took place. She'd been there too, I hadn't. She asked me if I had even walked the Freedom Trail. Surely I had, but I hadn't. By now, Ann must have been wondering what I had done in the first twenty-four years of my life and I was beginning to wonder the same thing.

We arrived and found the city was active with drivers. As we came down the ramp off the highway, traffic slowed and I shifted to a lower gear. A car going to the airport pulled in front of us as it tried to merge into the Callahan tunnel. We crept along at a snail's pace. But within walking distance of our restaurant I saw a car up ahead pull out of its parking space.

"That Irish luck of yours continues, John."

"Well, I go to church too, you know. Maybe it's clean living."

"Maybe it is or maybe it isn't."

As I reached around the back of Ann's headrest to park the car, I felt a few strands of her hair and got a scent of her perfume. The streetlight was right above us creating shadows and as I backed up I could sense she was looking at me—looking at me in a way that suggested she liked what she saw, that she felt comfortable and safe in my presence. But I sensed she was taking this brief moment to notice the physical me too, the distinctive chin with the cleft in the middle, the brown hair thinning at the top, and the sky-blue eyes.

"So where are you taking me to dinner?"

"Durgin Park. Ever been there?"

"I haven't. I heard the food was great and the waitresses insult you. Is that right?"

"Yes on both accounts."

Maybe it was the hug I'd given her back at her apartment that broke the ice, because as we left the car I reached for her hand to hold and was given no resistance. And as we walked we bumped shoulders a time or two and laughed for no reason at all.

After we were seated and had tasted our first glass of wine, I decided to go further.

"Ann, may I have a kiss?"

She gave me a puzzled look. "You mean right here, right now, in front of everyone?"

"Yes, right here right now and I don't care who is looking. I would like to kiss you."

I rose from my chair, keeping my knees bent. I leaned forward slowly, never taking my eyes off her. She smiled at me, then looked around at the other tables as if to carefully observe that no one was taking notice of us. She looked back at me and smiled again. Then she rose from her chair, leaned in close, cupped her hand on my chin, closed her eyes, and kissed me.

With that kiss, my red light turned green and I found myself on a different road.

"May I have another?"

Without wavering, she kissed me again, and the second was even better than the first. Moist and tender was this kiss.

"All right, John, let's sit down now before we make a scene."

"I enjoyed that, Ann. Did you?"

She tilted her head just like I had seen her do before and was blushing, but still smiling. I gathered from this that publicly displaying affection was probably not something Ann was comfortable with. Maybe behind closed doors in the proper setting at the proper time, but not in front of strangers. It probably wasn't done back in Darien. But I think she liked the spontaneity and I think she liked the kiss too. I may not have walked the Freedom Trail or climbed Bunker Hill, but at this moment I gave Ann something she needed: to feel pretty, to feel wanted, and to feel like she meant something to someone. And most of all to know that she was capable of touching a man's heart in a way she wasn't sure she could.

"Yes, John, I enjoyed it very much."

With that kiss, my red light turned green and I found myself on a different road.

May 1983

4 | LOVE

I fell in love with Ann over and over again, every time she touched me, every time she smiled, every time she laughed, every time she hugged her dad and kissed her mom.

By the time autumn had merged with winter, Ann and I were in love. It crashed into our lives at a speed neither one of us had ever felt before. We welcomed it with open arms as if we were welcoming home an old friend who had long escaped our sight.

We did everything together. We went to Cape Cod and took long walks along the shoreline on compressed sand, holding hands and looking for the perfect sea shell. We would debate over which shell was the best, claiming the others were not as perfectly shaped or were not as pretty or shiny. Eventually I would always admit defeat, but only after I was assured of a kiss. We'd take long rides to New Hampshire admiring the beauty of autumn in New England. She took me to the site of the famous tea party and I finally walked the Freedom Trail. Best of all, when doing nothing at all and for no apparent reason other than the joy in knowing we had each other, we laughed.

By Christmas, Ann wanted to take me back to her roots, back to the country in upstate New York. She had lived about half her life off the beaten track in this small town of Darien. Life was simple then and years later it remains so: a slower pace, no fences to keep people out, and everyone is welcome. The roads are straight, boxing in farms, and there is always a cool breeze in your face.

She waited until I was strapped in and the plane had pushed back from the Logan Airport terminal to tell me things about her family that to this point had gone unmentioned for reasons only Ann knew. For me, this was my first plane ride of my life.

"Babe," she began, because that's what we were now affectionately calling one another. "There is something I need to tell you about my family."

"Annie, can this wait until we are airborne? I'm nervous enough as it is."

I tried to be calm on the outside, but my moist palms gave away the butterflies that were flying around on the inside. I sat stone-faced, strapped in my seat as the engines began to roar and we gained speed down the runway. As we lifted off over the Atlantic, we quickly banked to the left and I wondered if that was normal. For a minute or two it seemed as if we were flying sideways. Ann sat calmly in the seat next to me, trying not to laugh. We headed west.

"All right, John, enough is enough. I know this is your first flight and all, but I need to tell you about my sister." Ann's impatience was noteworthy as I still squirmed in my seat. "You see, she's not real pleasant. In fact, it's like she's never happy. You'll see for yourself, but I wanted to warn you about her."

"You waited to tell me this after the plane took off? Did you think I was going to change my mind and get off the plane?"

"I just wanted you to be warned, so now you are."

"What's her problem?"

"Me."

"You are her problem?"

"Arlene has epilepsy. She has uncontrollable seizures. She is on medications that have a million side effects, and she has always wanted what I have. She doesn't work or can't work, I'm really not sure which it is. I think she could do something. I feel sorry for her, but I think she expects everything to be given to her and that's not the way life is. I just wish she wasn't always angry, especially toward me. Anyway, it'll be all right, but I didn't want you to be blindsided."

Buffalo was cold and windy. They talked of more snow. Either a few inches or a few feet, it all depended how the wind blew off the lake. As we descended, the pilot announced that due to wind conditions, we would have a choppy landing and we had to stay buckled in our seats.

"Buffalo is like this, John, cold and windy. I hope you can get used to this."

"That implies you'll be inviting me back here."

"Yes, it does, doesn't it?"

"What if I don't want to come back?"

"Then you'll be a fool."

Upon landing, we seemed to bounce a few times, but I could feel the brakes come on and the reverse thrusters engage, and I knew we had safely returned to earth.

The welcoming committee consisted of one man: Arnie Swable, Ann's dad. He was a veteran of the Korean War, and had a well-worn face wrinkled from the toil and sweat from serving his country and his family. According to what Ann said about him on the plane, he tended to say little, but said just enough to let you know he was listening. He parted his hair just above his left ear, with a few wisps trying to do the impossible. Arnie had never earned much money, but he never needed much either. He woke most mornings before sunrise, grabbed his lunch bucket, and out the door and off to work he went. His family always had a warm home to live in and enough food to eat. He worked as a carpenter, building new homes and making old ones better places to live. He pounded nails, cut wood, smoked his cigarettes down to the nub, and would often extinguish them with his calloused fingers. From Arnie, Ann learned her work ethic and mental toughness.

After a warm embrace shared between father and daughter, Ann introduced us.

We shook hands and exchanged greetings. His hard and calloused hand grasped mine. His face had character lines that stretched from his forehead to his chin.

"Good trip?" asked Arnie.

"Not too bad, a little bumpy. This was John's first plane ride, Dad, and he was a nervous wreck. Can you believe that? He's twenty-four years old and never been on a plane before!"

Ann poked me in the ribcage trying to get a laugh out of me.

"I thought I did very well, actually, until the winds kicked up and it felt like we were getting tossed around like a kite."

We retrieved our bags and as we stepped outside, the frigid air brushed up next to my exposed skin and for an instant I was stunned at how cold it was.

"Welcome to Buffalo, John," said Ann.

The snow had yet to come, but the wind seemed to chase us home, howling alongside the windows of Arnie's old Buick. Ann sat in the back seat and watched Arnie and me make the kind of small conversation you have with someone you've just met and don't know.

Just off the interstate we passed Pembroke Central.

"Babe, that's my old high school."

It was dark, but I turned and glanced through Arnie's window and for a moment thought of Ann in high school. I wondered again how we met, but I was grateful that we did. My mind paused for a moment and was wrapped up in an image of Ann in class, gazing out the window toward her future and wondering what her life would be like. Where was that man who would sweep her off her feet? How many children would she have? Where would she live? Would she be a nurse as she wanted to be or something else?

"I imagine it's much smaller than your high school, John."

Pulled out of my musings, I replied, "Probably so, Ann."

The ride was only about thirty minutes. We pulled into a one-car garage, unloaded the luggage, and came in from the cold. Ann's mom, Joyce, waited for us in the breezeway and gave Ann a big hug and a kiss. I could hear her telling Ann she missed her. Then she extended her hand to me.

"It's nice to finally meet you, John. Ann has told me so much about you. Welcome to our little country home. How was your first flight?"

"Fine, a little bumpy, I didn't know planes bounced when they landed."

The house was smaller than I imagined. It consisted of a tiny kitchen, one small bathroom, and three small bedrooms, but had a large family room with dark, paneled walls where the Christmas tree was lit up and the smell of pine filled the air. It felt lived-in to me—clean and comfortable, like an old T-shirt after it has just come from the wash and been hung out to dry in the fresh air. It was warm and I could smell the oil burner working overtime to keep it that way. I could see how Joyce made this house into a home for her family. The country décor and the smell of apple pie made this space inviting and charming.

Ann introduced me to her brothers, Aaron and Burt. They towered over me—I now knew what was meant by the term "big country boys."

Joyce smiled as she looked over her brood. "Did you know, John, when these kids were teenagers, Ann was half the size of Aaron, here?"

"He's older than Ann, right?"

"He is. And a big strapping football player he was, too, with legs the size of tree trunks and a belly that folded over his belt. But I knew when Ann was young, that for some reason she was different than her siblings. I didn't think the country would hold Annie." Apparently the simplicity of Darien was not what Ann wanted. The quiet was too quiet and the excitement Ann sought was just around the bend in the road, but not here. Not in Darien. Ann's magnet faced outward.

"Yet, at the same time," Joyce went on, "come the age when many teenagers got into trouble out in the cornfields drinking beer sold to them illegally or driving recklessly down a country road, Ann didn't. She stayed at home and knitted patchwork quilts with the idea that they would keep someone else warm during the long, cold Buffalo winters." I was finding out that she was selfless like that: always thinking of someone else before herself. Joyce went on to describe how she had taught Ann everything she knew about making quilts and sewing, and oftentimes they did this together. Purposeful work. Ann never understood why anyone would waste time doing crazy things. For her, every day had purpose and meaning. They talked about things mothers and daughters talked about. They talked about life beyond Darien, about children Ann might have one day. Ann hoped she'd have a daughter to teach how to sew and craft, to make patchwork quilts with.

After Ann's brothers and I exchanged handshakes and smiles, I caught sight of Arlene out of the corner of my eye. She was sitting on the couch knitting something, but looked intently at me. She never got off the couch and seemed to want me to come to her.

"Hi Arlene, this is John," Ann said.

"Hi Arlene, it's nice to meet you," I replied.

"Hi. I bet Ann has said a lot about me."

"A little bit, not too much."

"Well, you don't look much like the pictures I saw."

"Is that good or bad?"

"I don't know really, you just don't. You look older in person and I thought you were taller."

Throughout our conversation, Arlene never smiled. She kept knitting while we talked. I thought she looked nothing like Ann. She was much heavier and I imagined that had something to do with her medications. Her eyes were like black ice, pupils fully dilated, remaining dark and distant looking.

Ann and I unpacked. Joyce showed me around and made me feel at home. She had made cookies for me, so I got some milk and had a snack. I went into the family room where everyone else was gathered and almost on cue, Arlene had a seizure. I stared at her as she flailed away at her nose and made sounds I'd never heard before. I looked at Ann and Joyce thinking they would do something to help. Nothing was done at all and as soon as it started it was over.

"That was a mild one, John. We don't worry about them. She'll be fine."

We all hung out in the family room for a while and watched TV and made getting-to-know-you conversation. Joyce seemed to talk enough for all of us and we just filled in when she was catching her breath. But what a joy she was on my first visit to her home. I felt so welcomed and I could see where Ann got her beautiful features from.

My bed for the next few nights was in the living room on a pullout sofa. The metal coils poked my ribs, and I couldn't go to sleep until everyone else did, which was usually after the news. The bay window was just an arm's length away from me and when the lights dimmed I could see the wind and the snow mixing. I wondered what a portrait I would wake to in the morning. Joyce and Arnie slept right behind me. Down the short hallway, Ann slept in her old bedroom in her old bed next to Arlene. It was like they were children again.

But after everyone was tucked away for the night, Ann visited me. In the darkness of the room she snuggled in close. I put my arm around her; she rested her head on my shoulder, her hair so thick and beautiful, strands catching the bottom of my lip. She put her hand on my stomach and we talked in whispered tones as the wind whistled outside.

"So, John O'Shaughnessy, what do you think of my family?"

"They are all very nice, Annie. I like them and I hope they will like me."

"Just be yourself and they will. Things aren't real complicated here. We appreciate the simple things in life, so don't try to be someone you're not."

"I like that, because I only know how to be me."

"I am sorry about Arlene."

"What's there to be sorry about? She is not well and I feel sorry for her just like you do. I would not want to be her."

"You're right, but you know she is one of the reasons I had to leave here. I never liked the tension between us. It wore on me. I had to get away from that."

"I can understand that, but you don't have to apologize for her. She's your sister and the only one you'll ever have. You two are just very different but you must love each other."

"I suppose we do, we are sisters."

"Annie, I love you."

Ann lifted her head from my shoulder, looked me in the eyes, then closed hers. She reached in and gently kissed me. She pulled away, smiled, then hugged me and said, "I love you too, John O'Shaughnessy."

I am so grateful you are in my life, Annie. I feel we could be starting something pretty special here, you and me.

"I am so grateful you are in my life, Annie. I feel we could be starting something pretty special here, you and me. I know we have only known each other for a few months, but I think we complement each other. Do you know what I mean?"

"I do, babe, I do."

"Do you think your family likes me?"

"What's not to like? I know my mom likes you, she told me so, but she thought you looked older than twenty-four. I told her to get used to the fact that I was dating an older man. My dad doesn't say much, but if I asked him, and I will, I think he'll say he likes you."

"Well, I hope they all do. I feel comfortable here, like I belong."

"So does that mean you'll be coming back?"

"You knew I would."

"I hoped you would like it here. I never counted on it though. You're not from the country; this is a much slower pace. My family isn't as sophisticated as yours. I wasn't sure how you would react to it all, or even how they would react to you."

"Well, I am fine with everything. I can feel the slower pace and I kind of like it, maybe not to live here or anything. But to visit is okay."

We were both feeling the effects of the day and sleep was beginning to bring heaviness to our eyes. Having Ann next to me was all I needed. Blankets were unnecessary, her warmth was fine. The house was quiet and I stared outside into the dark night listening to the wind and listening to Ann. The long day, the plane ride, the wind, and the cold were cumulative things, and soon the heaviness we felt could no longer be ignored.

Christmas Eve morning, everyone in the house woke one by one to a beautiful country scene of pristine white snow a few inches deep, with drifts far larger. It looked like vanilla icing swirled on a cake and even if I wanted to remain in bed a while longer it would have been like trying to sleep in the middle of an intersection. So like everyone else, I got up.

"Good morning, John," said Joyce. "Do you drink coffee?"

"I can't do much until I have that first cup. The first one always tastes the best, doesn't it? The second cup is all right, but that first cup is heaven. Put me in for two or three."

"It's nice to have someone else to drink coffee with. No one else but me drinks it here." She flipped a switch on the coffee maker. "So, Ann has been telling me a lot about you. I know she loves Boston so much. I miss her, but I am glad that she is happy in the big city. Like I said last night, I knew she wouldn't stay here forever. She said this was your first plane ride."

"Yes, hard to believe I am twenty-four years old and never been on a plane. My parents didn't take us too many places and we always drove wherever we went. I don't remember too many big vacations; I think we went to Cape Cod a few times and the lakes of New Hampshire, always around water."

"Well, I haven't traveled much either. No, just kind of stayed here in the country. I like it here, it's quiet and nice, kind of simple, but that's okay too."

Ann checked in on us every now and then, but mostly let Joyce and me get acquainted. I enjoyed watching Ann in her childhood home. I glanced through photo albums and saw Ann growing up before my eyes. Joyce proudly narrated and it was like I was watching a black-and-white movie of the first twenty-five years of her life. It moved quickly from baby Ann, to big sister Ann, to cheerleader Ann, to nurse Ann. She smiled in every picture.

Joyce stuffed me like a turkey. Breakfast, lunch, and dinner, and all the chocolate chip cookies I could eat. We ate a beef on salty buns and poured gravy over it all. She baked pies from scratch—any kind I wanted. If I'd stayed long enough, I would have needed bigger clothes.

During the course of my stay in Darien, New York, I fell in love with Ann over and over again. It happened every time she looked at me, every time she touched me, every time she smiled, and every time she laughed. Every time she hugged her dad and kissed her mom. Every time she shadowboxed her little brother. And every time she did nothing at all but be herself.

I thought there was something magical going on here, and even though Ann and I had only known each other three short months, I had seen and felt enough, and on Christmas Day, I knew something no one else knew. The remark I made to my mother that I would "never find my future wife in a bar" was all a lie, and I knew there was only one thing left for me to do.

5 | A LILY IN THE FIELD

Ann overlooked my imperfections and I admired hers.

The cold and the darkness of winter had given me plenty of time to stay inside where it was warm and plan my next move. I knew what I wanted to do. I knew I wanted to marry Ann. More than anything I wanted that, but I wanted this joyous feeling to settle over me like a warm wool blanket. I wanted to slow things down, making sure I wasn't dreaming any of this. I wanted to let the driftwood dry out a little, enjoy my new surroundings, take it all in the moment that it was.

I wasn't impulsive enough to just pop the question when the moment felt right. The moment had felt right almost from the first time we ever spoke. It felt even more right after the Freedom Trail ride when she showed me around my own city answering questions before I asked them. At Thanksgiving at my parents' house, she glowed; it felt right then, too. But home in the country was when I really knew for sure. I could have asked her right then and there in front of Joyce and Arnie, but that moment wasn't right either. Besides, I thought, this was forever, what was the hurry?

So the real question was, what did I know about diamonds? The only answer I knew was that they were expensive, some more than others, and they all glistened, some more than others, but I really was lost when it came to this engagement thing. Ann wasn't pretentious and I knew she wouldn't want me to buy some rock that had an extended payment plan. I felt comfortable that whatever I picked out she'd love. So it came down to the fact that I was doing this more for me than for her. I wanted her to love the ring for the meaning behind it, not for the clarity in it.

So I shopped. All over in fact: department stores, jewelry stores, diamond brokers. All the time I spent looking for her special ring, she may have wondered if I had someone else on the side. Shopping for the perfect diamond was hard work, but she was worth it.

I wanted to let the driftwood dry out a little, enjoy my new surroundings, take it all in the moment that it was.

By the time I'd saved enough money and found her ring, it was almost Easter. The ground was still moist from melted snow and the scent of mist and mud was in the air. Green was replacing brown as the color of nature. The breezes were warmer now and the sun seemed nearer. Nothing had changed between Ann and me. More in love maybe, more attached, and more committed too.

A lily in the field she was.

We never fought, never argued. Ann never pushed, she pulled; she led.

I followed—willingly.

"What do you have there?"

"Can I get a hello first and maybe a kiss?" As I entered Ann's apartment, she impatiently pecked my lips like she was kissing a baby, not her future husband.

"Hello, John, now why the Easter basket? Is there any chocolate in there?"

"Nope, no food, just some poems I wrote."

"Give me another kiss," she said, and then with that distraction, like a thief in the night, she swiped the basket from my reach. I followed her as we walked to her living room. We rested on her sofa and she opened each egg, reading the poems back to me.

You are my sunshine,
You are my world,
You are my life,
You are my only girl.

She looked at me. "A little cheesy maybe, but I love it."

Love is so rare; one will often spend a lifetime in aimless pursuit.
I am so fortunate to have found someone as rare as love itself.

"I really like that one, John."

You make my world a special place to be and my life a special life to live.

"Very cute, John. Now give me a big kiss."
"You have one more to go, you know."
"I know, I saved the pink one for last. What does this poem say?"
Buried beneath the grass and inside the pink egg she saw something sparkle and it was then she knew it was no poem. She looked at me with a gleeful smile and before digging any further she put the basket down.
"Is this what I think it is? Are you sure, John?"
"Ann, I have never been surer of anything in my life. I love you and I want to spend my life with you, the rest of my life with you."
She searched through the manufactured grass and retrieved the ring from the egg and tried to blink away her tears. "Oh, John, I can't believe this!"
I knelt down on one knee, on the creaky hardwood floor, and temporarily removed the ring from Ann's grip. I looked up and saw the tears could no longer be contained.
"Ann, will you marry me?"
She leaped at me like a frog leaping on a lily pad and wrapped her arms around my neck. My rear end crashed into the floor creating a loud

thud that shook the room and everything in it. With this move we found ourselves horizontal, our eyes, noses, and mouths crushed up against one another, creating an exciting but unfocused view. We went with the moment, closed our eyes, and, turning our heads in opposite directions, pressed our lips together and kissed. While still locked in each other's arms, Ann whispered in my ear.

"John, I have never loved anyone like I love you. You have just made me the happiest girl in the world. My answer is YES!" She then jumped to her feet and extended out her left hand to me. "Now put it on, I want to see it on my finger."

Trying to reconfigure my spine, I rose more cautiously than Ann and placed the ring on her trembling left hand.

"It's beautiful. I love it. It fits perfectly, did pick this out yourself?"

"I did. I am glad you love it. I was a little worried."

She sat down, then placed her left hand on her right knee and admired

The driftwood that I was for so many years had found a new home on dry land: Ann's sandy beach.

it. Extending her hand in the air she watched it glisten against the sun's rays that entered through the sole window in the room.

"I love it and I love you. I can't believe this is happening. I am getting married! I'm getting married to you. I need to call people, my mom, Laureen, Kathy. You need to call your mom and dad. Do they know?"

"Yes, they do. They are excited for us."

"Did you ask my dad for my hand?"

"I wasn't that old-fashioned. Besides, I knew the answer."

At that moment, Good Friday, 1982, the driftwood that I was for so many years had found a new home on dry land: Ann's sandy beach. I had never been so happy, nor had she. We seemed the perfect complement to each other. She was patient, I wasn't. I broke things, she fixed them. I was a spender, she saved. She overlooked my imperfections and I admired hers.

We remained inseparable, but I moved back home to save some money to help pay for the wedding and the marriage, the price of love. Every night I ventured home, Ann would pout, stomp her feet, and cry when it was time for me to go. She feared I would never make it home, that I would be killed by a drunken driver. She feared that in that instant, her life would be changed forever. Before I could escape, she would always grab me around the waist, look up at me all teary-eyed, and give me advice for the ride home.

"John, please drive safely and look both ways."

"I will, Annie, I'll see you tomorrow. Give me a kiss."

I made it home safely every night and made it back into her arms every day. For much of the year after that, Ann was very busy planning her big day. I offered as much help as was needed, but basically did as I was told. The less I did, the better the chances were for a splendid wedding. She gave me one job, pick the band. We had engagement photos taken and Joyce and Arnie proudly posted their daughter's wedding announcement in the local paper. The big day was May 14, 1983.

On May 14, 1983, at half past five, we were married. It was a Saturday. Ann felt lucky that day and bought a lottery ticket. 4-5-9-12-14-30. She didn't win. She chose white calla lilies and a beautiful white lace wedding dress, size four. The bridesmaids wore pink taffeta gowns and the grooms-men classic black tuxes. Mine had a long tail. My best man was my eldest brother, Jim. We celebrated that day. Toasts were made in our honor and people expressed hope for a lifetime filled with health and happiness. I gave a speech and thanked everyone for helping to make this day and my life so special.

Ann and I honeymooned in Bermuda. It was magical. Strangers snapped pictures of the two of us wearing short shorts and silly hats as we stood under old trees that dotted the landscape. We walked through botanical gardens, and through a glass bottom boat we could see the remains of a sunken ship just off the coast. We enjoyed champagne parties and delicious meals. We capped off many an evening with a round of strip poker, then making love.

In 1983, the world was tense. A South Korean Boeing 747 bound for Seoul was shot down by a Soviet fighter jet after it strayed into Soviet air space, killing 269 passengers. In Beirut, 237 U.S. Marines were killed by a terrorist bomber. President Reagan was planning an invasion of the island of Grenada to rescue American medical students. We, on the other hand, were oblivious to all that was going on around us. I moved in with Ann. Our mattress was on the floor and I had to be careful not to stand up too quickly or I would crack my head on the overhanging ceiling. My closet was in my office right by the clock on my desk that was a constant reminder of our love. The shower was in an old tub with an ugly vinyl curtain. It took several minutes for warm water to flow through the old pipes. The water was dangerous. An old tannery not far from the town's water supply had leaked chemicals into the well. People here were dying of cancer.

We were doing what most young married couples did; we frolicked. We didn't have any troubles. We ate pizza and drank beer. We watched television on a thirteen-inch black-and-white; it sat precariously on a brown end table that most people would have thrown to the curb a long time ago. We took long walks and talked about babies. We picked out a name, Katie Ann.

Dear Mr. and Mrs. O'Shaughnessy,

It's already Wednesday and I have yet to come out of the clouds. What a weekend of beautiful memories.

As I look back on the past twenty-five years of my life I can recall comments like, "you'll never marry," and "you're too fussy." "What are you looking for, he was a nice guy." "No one will ever be good enough for you." That's right, I was the one who wanted to marry because I truly loved someone and wanted to share the rest of my life with that one person. Marriage to me wasn't to be entered into lightly and I know people who wed because they "get along."

I always wanted to be a wife and a mother, but so many factors had to be right. I am telling you all this because I want you to see how special John is to me. He possesses so many qualities that mean so much to me. John always says "Annie, the little things make you so happy." They always have and always will. John has high values that come from you and the way you raised him. You can be proud of him. His manners, charm, intelligence, and looks all reflect upon both of you.

I will do all I can to make him happy. I realize marriage is a give-and-take relationship. I feel both of us have seen this in our parents. It's not all a bed of roses and we must both work at it together. John once told me, "Annie, my family doesn't know the meaning of divorce." Nothing could have pleased me more.

I have felt so welcomed into your family and that means everything to me. I told my mother about yours and my mom was very pleased because she is so far away from us. I am looking forward to a growing loving relationship with all of the O'Shaughnessys.

Thank you for being there with the warmth and wishes on my special weekend. Thank you for your blessings.

Love,

Ann

6 | THE FAMILY

You're a hero today and a bum tomorrow.

Uncle Bill Flynn

Married life agreed with me. Was there any doubt it would? I think it was the connectedness that I liked, the tethered string. It was like the tide and the rocks, ebbing and flowing, mercurial, but always linked to each other, never straying far. A slate wiped clean each day, with lasting memories tucked away in the vastness.

Ann's genius was that she made me think I wanted all the same things she did. Her favorite colors became mine and I wondered all these years how I ever liked the color blue, when green was so much prettier. The furniture she bought—"You're gonna love it," she'd say to me as the delivery men would come waltzing though the front door with a new green couch. And the weekend getaways she'd plan for the two of us at just the right time as if she knew, and I suppose she did, that we both

It was like the tide and the rocks, ebbing and flowing, mercurial, but always linked to each other, never straying far.

needed some alone time.

Everything seemed to move at a nice pace, in measured steps that I could count on. A master plan that I knew nothing about, but nonetheless was a part of. We were working this plan together, one brick at a time, walking in each other's footsteps, learning what we liked and didn't like, making adjustments along the way. It was not without effort and neither of us was perfect, but these early days of our marriage seemed to come naturally to Ann and me.

After two years of marriage, we bought our first house. We went courting this house long after dark. For all we knew, the back yard could have been piled with dead horses. One room we couldn't enter because a baby was in there sleeping and dreaming. It was small and one hopes that a first house could be grander in scale. I was no different, but Ann was and she loved this little house with the mysterious back yard. An offer was already pending so we had to move quickly. We offered the sellers more than they were asking and, quite frankly, more than we could afford. The house was ours.

The back yard didn't have anything dead or fermenting there, it was just large; a lot to mow, I thought. And in a flicker, the walls were green, the carpet was green, and the couch was green. All in measured steps that I unwittingly approved of, perhaps in the shower or in my sleep. She was something like that.

And after everything was painted green and we were on firm footing, it was time to make babies.

At Christmas time I was given my initial introduction to our first child. It kicked me. I had just got finished kissing Ann's stuffed belly when a little knob popped through her skin, for just a second and then retreated into her warm womb. We laughed and waited, waited and laughed, but our baby went back to sleep all tired out from its little kick. I referred to our little person now as the "little boot."

As Ann was glowing in her pregnancy, my uncle, Bill Flynn, learned he had lung cancer. He was my mother's brother and my favorite uncle. He had smoked his unfiltered cigarettes his whole life but now he was paying the price. He was dying. Like me, Uncle Bill had sold food for a living. Bill once told me to remember one thing.

"John, you're a hero today and a bum tomorrow."

In that one sentence Bill Flynn summed up one of life's greatest lessons. Stay humble. Stay grounded. You're not as good as you think you are. I remember him saying that to me in his gruff raspy voice like it was yesterday.

He'd always ask me who I was dating too. He had names for every nationality. One time he said I was dating a "rug merchant." I knew he was a bigot, but if there was such a thing as a nice bigot, that was Uncle Bill.

Ann did glow. She loved being pregnant. She loved the feeling of a little person growing inside her. The changes she felt every day, changes that only a mother could understand and appreciate. If anyone was born to be a mother, it was Ann.

I loved our new home, especially the basement. It was my domain. It had white-pine tongue-and-groove paneling and a brown remnant carpet left over from when we changed the upstairs carpet to teal green. It was small but manly, and large enough for a couch, a table, a television, and a gas-powered space heater the size of a stove. Ann hated it. It was too cold and drafty. With my new company, I had won a contest for selling the largest display of canned vegetables. It was as large as the Green Giant himself. The prize was a brand new twenty-four-inch RCA color television that sat on a swivel. I loved this new TV, and from this spot I would watch the Boston Celtics win another championship and the Red Sox break my heart for another year.

I knew if Ann was coming downstairs, it wasn't to join me. It usually meant I had chores to do that were now several days past due. The honeymoon was long over and we had become a married couple. She would kindly remind me of my chores and like a fool, I would kindly negotiate for more time. It never worked. Now

One person dies, while another is born.

and then she might bring me a beer, perhaps as a reward for doing one of my chores on time, but more often than not, I got it myself. I heard her walking upstairs, she was now waddling a bit, her belly in full bloom. She had just hung up the phone. The walk sounded different. It was.

"John, that was your mom who called." Ann paused a moment before giving me the news I didn't want to hear. "Uncle Bill just died."

She hugged me. Well, at least tried to hug me. The little boot was in the way. We basically hugged faces. Ann knew I had lost more than an uncle, I had lost a hero. I thought my dear old uncle was making room for the little boot.

One person dies, while another is born.

On Palm Sunday, the sun blinked through some overhanging clouds and it was that time in New England when the grass was still dormant and the perennials were just beginning to awaken from a long winter's slumber. On Saturday, Ann raked two bags of leaves, the last remnants of the previous autumn. She woke up early that morning, her back aching from the weight of carrying the little boot. It was almost eight o'clock and I was still fast asleep when Ann bent over my head and whispered a wake-up call in my ear.

"John," she murmured, nudging my shoulder. "John, you need to wake up."

I squinted through my eyelids, threw my pillow over my head, and in muffled words asked, "What time is it?"

"It's time for you to be a daddy."

"WHAT!" My eyes sprang wide open.

"My water just broke; we need to go to the hospital, like now."

"Are you sure, Annie?"

"John, of course I'm sure. Now get moving and put these clothes on."

I sat up on the side of the bed, looked down at my bare feet, scratched the side of my head, and thought what an amazing day this was going to be.

Our son, Eric Jon, the little boot, was born on March 23, 1986. Eric was two weeks early and he only weighed six and a half pounds. A tiny lad he was. For me, it was painless until Ann hit me in the head screaming for an epidural . . . "NOW!" Oh, the things we do for love.

And what a spectacle it was. A tiny seed and egg had become a sea of confusion and pain. She held my hand until my fingers turned blue, but dare I say I was in pain? I didn't have a watermelon between my legs. The push, the pull, the turning, the squeezing, and then a spank and a cry, there he was, this little seed and little egg had become a little man: our little man.

Eric and Mom would come home three days later on March 26. Ann thought Eric was skinny as "chicken bones" and actually wanted to send him back to the hospital. He was, after all, two weeks ahead of schedule and it would take a little time to put some meat on his little bones. We didn't send him back, we loved him, and every day he got a little bigger.

Ann kept a first-year calendar.

March 30	First shampoo.
March 31	Dad returns to work, we miss him.
April 1	Big day, umbilical cord falls off.
April 3	We visit Dad at work. Eric was a hit.
April 5	Grandma Swable comes to visit— "he's so small."
April 25	You did a big smile to Mommy today. You have your first cold—sneezing a lot.
May 1	Now ten pounds, four ounces.
May 10	We bought a rocking chair.
May 21	You slept through the night for the first time.
June 5	You begin to creep.
June 14	Responding to environment.
June 18	You snore for the first time.
August 10	Dad now calls you "boot monster."
August 16	We went shopping—you were great.

On and on it went. In November, Eric was pulling himself up and speaking his first words: "da da." That was my boy. At Christmas, we flew to New York so his grandparents could spoil him. Not even one year old, and he was flying! By February, we all flew to Florida to visit my parents at their winter home. Ann and I got away to Disney World for some personal time. It was fabulous and we planned another trip when we all could come.

The first year with Eric went quickly. He was a great baby boy with big hazel eyes like his mom that dominated his little face. By the time he could walk, he would waddle his little body over to the front window, prop himself up on his Little Tikes stool, and on Mom's cue he would wait for me to come home. As he saw my car turn the corner, he would turn to mom and say "da, da, da," and dance around the living room with one hand raised. He was so excited that I was home. I gave him a huge hug, spun him around the room, gave his little belly raspberries, and we all laughed.

I enjoyed watching Ann become a wonderful mother. For her it was instinctual. It was what she was born to do. Being a wife and a mother were the things she wanted to do most in life. She was in her glory and I had never seen her as happy as she was at this moment when Eric was just a peanut and we were a family, her family.

While I was a loving dad, Ann attended Eric's every need. She knew the sounds of each noise, when he was hungry, sleepy, or just plan cranky, which wasn't often. I would sit in the back seat for a while, but that was all right, as I was able see the bond that was being nurtured between Ann and her son.

She earned money being a nurse, but her reward in life was being a mother.

Ann's career was alive and well, but clearly her family came first. She worked weekends. Her patients missed her working full time but understood she was now a young mother and perhaps she reminded some of the elderly women of themselves many years before. Every break she had, she found time to call home to check in on Eric and me.

"Is he all right?'

"Did you change him?"

"What did he eat?"

"When did he eat?"

"Did he nap?"

"How long did he nap?"

The mother in Ann never took any time off. Being needed by this little person, making sure he was well, protecting him from the world: that was now her true joy in life. I knew that.

I always wanted my boys to remain small, but they grew. I missed holding them in their one-piece terry-cloth suits. They both looked so cute.
A Mother's Journal
August 1995
Ann O'Shaughnessy

Ann and baby Eric, sound asleep on the green sofa in 1986.

7 | THE SALESMAN

It was no coincidence that my career began to blossom after I had settled down with a woman I loved. There was something comforting about having a safe haven to come home to, a warm spot to climb into after a long day. Ann did that for me.

I'd always wanted to be an architect, not a salesman. As a youngster, I could sit for hours and draw up "blueprints" of my dream house. All I needed was some graph paper, a pencil, and a ruler. I'd even taught myself how to sketch, drawing in shadows under the gutters and darkness in the windows.

But to be a good architect, I needed to be good with math, and I wasn't. I abandoned my dream and became dreamless. I entered college to study business. I wanted to quit after the first semester. I was floundering. In my late teens and early twenties, I was just going through the motions expecting life to come to me.

I learned after a while, it didn't.

So I graduated, hardly with honors, but I did okay. Solid B, I guess. A sales job just seemed to earn its spot in my life by default, not by passion or determination. It just seemed like the thing for me to do. My father was in sales, as were my brother Tom, and Uncle Bill. Always food sales: "Everyone has to eat," my dad would say.

So I started at the bottom with a food broker. My first year, I made about $11,000 with a car allowance. I thought I was rich, so at that point I bought that nice white sports car that drove like the wind. I'd go to the stores, dust off my cans of tuna, try to steal some additional real estate on the shelves and sell something to someone who treated me like I was a door-to-door vacuum salesman.

But it was a job.

I did that for about two years and then hit the big time when I landed a job with a national food company, Pillsbury. People called me the dough-boy. I got a big raise and a company car. Same job though, just different products to push.

One time at a national sales conference, the president of the company asked us all for suggestions on how we could make the company better.

I raised my hand.

"Why don't we put the doughboy on a diet?" I said.

The room of over three hundred suits went dead silent. You'd think I just killed the pudgy bastard. I struck a chord, a blasphemous, dissonant chord.

"Are you serious?" he replied.

"I am! People in the eighties are more health conscious. He stands for fattening foods. Just slim him down a little," I said.

"Does anyone else agree with this position?"

The room's occupants murmured a resounding "No."

I was willing to swim upstream, against the current, not afraid to step out and speak up.

But I learned something about myself. I learned I was willing to swim upstream, against the current, not afraid to step out and speak up. I learned I had a good head on my shoulders, because that was a damn good idea and I knew it, even if a room full of suits felt otherwise.

It was no coincidence that my career began to blossom after I had settled down with a woman I loved. There was something comforting about having a safe haven to come home to, a warm spot to climb into after a long day. Ann did that for me. She was the sounding board I needed and often changed the directions of my sails, sending me off with the wind at my back, full speed ahead.

And so it was, chasing a ghost the next few years we began moving all over the country. In Dallas, I became one of the youngest managers in the company at age twenty-nine. I managed people my father's age. In 1988, Ann and I had our second son, little Collin Patrick. Eric had a buddy to play with and Ann had another son to dote over. In Kansas City, I became the manager of one of our biggest accounts in the country, and in 1991, I won sales rep of the year. We now paid cash for cars and owned bigger homes.

But Uncle Bill tapped me on the shoulder from the grave. *John*, I could hear him saying to me, *you're a hero today and a bum tomorrow.* In 1992, I fell out of favor. I had superior performance reviews, awards. It made no sense. Maybe it was that doughboy remark after all, or maybe it was just politics. I wasn't fired, but I didn't feel wanted anymore either, so rather than letting them push me off the cliff, I jumped.

Soon, I found another job with more money and we got to move further north to Michigan. Life was good. Ann and I were getting older, with a few more aches and pains, but more in love than ever, the ebb and flow, the tethered string.

In Michigan I turned into a workaholic. I left home at seven am and if I was lucky, I returned at seven pm. Often, I ate dinner alone. I was learning my way around my new job and I had much to learn. I had more responsibility than I had ever dreamed of: sales, marketing, hiring, firing, profits, losses, market share, and reports. I loved my new job. I took work home with me and read through mail while we watched television on the twenty-four-inch RCA. I was determined to make the best of what I was offered. I was driven to climb the ranks in this new company and to never feel like I wanted to leave.

"Hey, remember me?"

"What do you mean?" I responded from my home office camped on the living room floor, shuffling through two-day-old mail.

"John, every night you come home with work. I look into your eyes and all I see is you thinking about work. What about me?"

I looked up at Ann and felt awful. My job had followed me home for over a year now and the sad part was I didn't even realize it. I was so caught up in being a success at work that I hadn't noticed I was failing at home. I closed my mail.

"Ann, I'm sorry. You're right, but I just don't want to ever feel like I failed again, so I work my ass off."

"You didn't fail, John. They failed you. Your old boss had just given you the highest rating you can get. You had just won that award. You were not a failure."

I had been ignoring Ann for months. She could have been mad and jealous, but instead she lifted me up. All she asked for was a little more attention. She knew I took my career seriously and gave me about a year to figure it all out, then it was time to be a family again. She patiently waited for me to return to her, and I did.

In our back yard one day, before the white picket fence began to crumble and the hours I worked didn't span half of the day, Eric found a new friend, a green frog. He named him Charlie and every day he would go outside and look for him. He lived in a hole in the ground under the tree. Eric would reach his little arm inside the hole and pull poor Charlie out and they would play in the dirt together. He'd chase him around the yard. Old Charlie couldn't jump fast enough to escape Eric. Collin would ask to see him and Eric would pick Charlie up and put him up close to Collin's eyes so Collin could study his bulging eyes and slimy reptilian skin. Eric would play with his new friend until it got dark and then he would ask Ann if he could bring Charlie inside. She always said "no."

Eric, Charlie the frog, a neighbor friend, and Collin.

8 | MOM IS BEAUTIFUL

It's the elements of nature that make the tree stronger: the sun, the cold, the heat, the rain, and the wind. A constant cycle of transformation, every day it digs in, fighting to survive.

Ann was taking more time than usual getting ready for our big night out on the town. It was our own fault for not going out more often, but the boys were the center of our world now. All of six and eight, little pumpkins they were, and we were okay with enjoying a movie and a bag of popcorn at home in our living room. We'd have friends over to play card games, and on special occasions like birthdays or anniversaries we'd find ourselves alone in a nice restaurant reminiscing on how we ever came to be.

This night was different and Ann was taking this opportunity to pamper herself. She took a long hot shower, letting the steam and hot water relax her muscles and take the soreness out of her shoulder. She laid out several outfits trying to put form and function together, finally settling on an appealing green and white dress. She blow-dried and curled her hair, paying attention to every detail, making sure it was as pretty as she wanted it to be. But she spent more time on her face than anything: the moisturizer, the blush, the mascara, the eyeliner, the lipstick. Ann was beautiful with or without makeup, but was nothing short of stunning with it.

"Mom, you look beautiful."

"Thank you, Collin. I feel beautiful, too. I want you and Eric to behave yourselves tonight. And bedtime is at ten pm sharp. Remember to take a shower before bed. Eric, did you hear me?"

"I did Mom, bed at eleven, shower at ten."

"Eric, that's not what I said and you know it."

"All right Mom, you and Dad have fun."

"Boys, come give me a kiss before I go."

Eric got up from the couch where he was watching television and ran into the kitchen, planting a big kiss on Ann's lips. Collin did the same. She gave out some final instructions to the babysitter and handed him the phone number for where we would be. She gave the boys another kiss and off we went.

You spend so much time and attention on your family I feel that sometimes you neglect yourself.

It was late autumn and darkness draped over us around dinner time, making the days short and the evenings long. We backed out of the driveway, then headed to downtown Detroit to a fundraising event for the American Cancer Society.

"Collin beat me to it, you know. You do look beautiful, Annie. I love it when you get all dressed up."

"Thanks, babe. This should be fun tonight, just you and me for a change. I hope the boys have fun too. You know how they like having a boy babysitter. I guess they get to do more rough stuff."

"Do you remember who we are meeting tonight?"

"Yes, I do. Gary and his wife Annette, Steve and April, John and Kathy. Am I right?"

"Perfect. By the way, how's that shoulder of yours?"

"It's okay."

"Are you sure?"

"Well I don't know, the steroid shot seemed to help for about a week or two, but it hurts again. Tylenol seems to help me a little. It gets me through the night so I can get some sleep."

"I can tell it hurts you. When do you see the doctor again?"

"I don't have an appointment. She said to only come back if the pain didn't go away."

"Well, did it?"

"I know. I should give her a call next week. Let's try to have fun tonight and not think about it."

"All right, but promise me you will call on Monday. Sometimes I worry about you. You spend so much time and attention on your family I feel that sometimes you neglect yourself."

"I promise, John. Enough with the shoulder talk; it's just bursitis, nothing more. Please don't worry."

We arrived at the Ren Cen in Detroit, a big tall glass building on the shores of the Detroit River, not far from Greektown. We were seated at our table, had gone through introductions, and had barely sliced into our salads when an official-looking man came to our table.

"Excuse me, is there a Mr. and Mrs. O'Shaughnessy at this table?"

Ann and I simultaneously looked up and I almost choked on a half-eaten cucumber. I knew something bad had happened. I raised my hand.

"Yes, that's us."

"The Plymouth police need to talk with you. Follow me and I will take you to a phone."

We both jumped from our chairs. On the way up, my knee hit the bottom of the table, causing waves in the water glasses. Our napkins fell to the floor.

"Please point to the phones," I asked.

"Through those doors and to the right, here is the number."

I snatched the piece of paper from his hand and ran straight for the doors. Ann walked quickly behind me, trying to control her emotions and thoughts about what might have happened. I fumbled in my pocket for money to make the call. I didn't have enough, so I used my calling card to get through. A woman answered the phone. Ann listened in to the phone with me.

"Hello, Plymouth police."

"Hello, this is John O'Shaughnessy, I was told to call you."

"Yes, Mr. O'Shaughnessy, we were expecting your call. There has been an accident. Your son Collin and his brother are being taken to St. Joseph's Hospital. You need to go there right away."

"What happened, are they okay?"

"All I know is Collin was injured in your front yard. He apparently broke his arm. I suggest you leave immediately."

"Was it just a broken arm or something more?

"I believe that was it."

"We are on our way."

We returned to our table. People could tell from the ashen looks on our faces that we would not be staying. We told them all we knew and gracefully departed, grabbing our coats and racing for the car and the hospital.

"John, tell me Collin is okay. What kind of babysitter lets this happen? He won't be babysitting our children again. I don't think this would have happened if a girl was watching them."

"It's just a broken arm, Annie, he'll be fine. I hope it's his left arm though, he's going to pitch with his right arm."

"John, our son is in pain in the hospital, and all you can think about is baseball?"

"I'm just saying, I hope it's his left arm, that's all."

"Please drive faster. He needs me."

Thirty minutes later we sped into the emergency area, tires screeching. "Drop me off here, John, you park the car."

I found Ann, Eric, and Collin behind curtains. The boys had been there for about an hour. Collin's arm was suspended by rope. His fingers were inserted into a suction-cup-like device with weights dangling from his elbow allowing gravity to stretch out his arm. His little left wrist was as crooked as an old branch. He looked terrified. Medicine relieved some of his pain. Ann stood next to Collin and caressed his forehead. I leaned over and kissed his warm cheek.

"How are you doing, pal?"

"Not too good, Dad. It's not my pitching arm, though."

Ann looked at me and rolled her eyes, a slight look of disdain directed at me. "Well, that's some good news," she said.

Eric tugged at my pants leg and looked up at me. "Dad, I rode in the ambulance with Collin. I got to ring the siren."

"You did? Did you help your brother during the ride?"

"Yeah, I told him it would be okay. The doctors will fix him up."

"Eric, what happened?" I asked.

"David was playing with Collin in the front yard. He threw him up in the air but didn't catch him right and Collin fell hard on his wrist. David's dad called 9-1-1."

Ann was now even more furious and so was I.

Young doctors in their late twenties hovered around Collin looking at X-rays. They kept looking at his wrist too, touching it and discussing options. Collin kept looking at them, wanting them to make his arm look normal again.

"It's a clean break," the doctor declared. "I need to reset it, but I don't think you want to be in the room when I do."

"John, I'm staying with Collin. Eric doesn't need to watch this, you take him with you."

Eric and I stepped out and within minutes, Collin's arm was straight again and wrapped in ACE bandages. A week later, it was placed in a hard cast and by the first snowfall it was all healed, good as new.

Ann's shoulder was another story. The pain persisted, as did my worries.

During the months of November and December, we played Nutcracker music and sang Christmas songs constantly and we made advent wreaths together. We made many ornaments and fun things. We loved doing things together.

A Mother's Journal

August 1995

Ann O'Shaughnessy

We are all wearing Christmas sweatshirts that Ann made for our first Christmas with the four of us in 1988. Ann, Collin, Eric, and me.

9 | THE NURSE

For Ann, the most important things in life could not be bought; they were made, like friendships and memories.

The end of Ann's childhood came in the spring of 1974 when she removed a mortarboard from her head and threw it up in the air. She watched it spin and turn, contrasting against the sky filled with cotton-ball clouds, landing safely near her feet. After sitting for hours on uncomfortable wooden chairs in alphabetized rows, listening to speeches she would soon forget, she had graduated from high school. She was an honors student, math was her favorite subject, and history was her best. Her future was bright. She could have written the class motto, *I have friends to discover and many things to understand.*

Many of Ann's classmates were done with school that day. Some were done long before that, but showed up anyway. They took respectable nine-to-five kinds of jobs that earned them a living—not much above minimum wage at the grocery store, the toll booth, or in fields baling hay.

Ann had other plans. Looking back, she felt a calling to be a nurse before her teen years and by the time she entered high school, it seemed to be a foregone conclusion. She had all the skills it took to be a good nurse: patience, compassion, and intelligence. And to get paid for helping people get over their injuries or ailments, or to help them deal with them peace-fully, made it all that more appealing to her.

Ann went back to school and eighteen months later received her LPN degree from Agricultural and Technical College in Morristown, New York. She found work at a hospital in nearby Batavia where she worked on the heart floor. It was there that she first began to work with older patients, many of whom had suffered heart attacks. She had already gone further in school than any of her siblings ever would, but still wanted more. She felt she was doing the work the RNs were doing, but was getting paid much less. Her confidence grew, but when she came home to tell her dad she wanted to go back to school, he couldn't understand why. He had never finished high school.

From the time Ann began her nursing career, and for most of her adult life, dying was a part of living. It was that way because of the type of nursing she chose to do: geriatric nursing. By the time Ann first met her patients, they were oftentimes in their seventies or eighties. Old age was catching up with them; they were breaking bones, they were forgetting things like their names, and they were developing illnesses that were slowly stripping them of everything they worked so hard all their lives to hold on to.

We only have the moment we now live in and that can be taken away at any time, and all this stuff we accumulate in our lives doesn't go with us when we're gone.

That's where Ann came in. Every morning when she arrived at the hospital, she'd make her rounds to all of her patients, letting each of them know that she was now on duty and if they needed anything, all they had to do was ring for her and she would be there for them in a flash. Ann would think, "How can I not serve these people in a dignified professional manner? They worked hard all their lives raising children, sweeping floors, paying bills, trying to keep marriages together, and now this." For some, all they had to look forward to was the smile on her face.

And so she smiled, letting them hold on to one last thing.

I think being a nurse helped to shape who Ann was. The circle of life was shown to her every day. It taught her something profound. It taught her that we only have the moment we now live in and that can be taken away at any time, and all this stuff we accumulate in our lives doesn't go with us when we're gone.

I'm pretty sure none of Ann's patients who were approaching their final hours ever said they wished they had bought another fancy car or a bigger boat. On the other hand, I imagined they were more humble and contrite and wished they'd spent more time with their kids, or they'd gone on more vacations, and that big house they had all those years was nice, but there was a lot of useless empty space that they never needed. Some may have said, "I wish I'd never smoked."

For Ann, the important things in life could never be bought, they were made, like friendships and memories.

In the fall of 1973, shortly after she'd begun her senior year at Pembroke Central High School, Ann was summoned to the principal's office to see Mr. Walline. She was horrified and her mind raced to things she might have done wrong. It came up empty. He asked Ann to enter the local Junior Miss pageant in a town called Le Roy. Though she was now relieved, she could not understand why he wanted her. To enter this she thought she needed a talent, and what was hers? Mr. Walline asked her, "Who drew the cartoons on all the walls in the school?"

"Well, I did." Ann replied.

"Then that's your talent."

Most of the girls danced, sang, played piano or guitar. Ann drew. She wore her cheerleader outfit with white knee-high socks and white saddle shoes. She sketched a life-size football caricature with glow-in-the-dark chalk. She did it live, just like the other girls. They dimmed the lights and when the football player lit up the stage, he said WIN.

Ann won too.

10 | In an Instant

*Comfort doesn't bring growth. Pain takes us out of our normal
existence and leads us to places we never thought we could go.
Through the hottest fire comes the finest steel.*

Of course, we didn't know it at the time, but in 1994, storm clouds
were forming off in the distance. Ann and I had been married
for eleven years now. Our sons were eight and six, best of friends,
and the lights in our lives. We had a home that was warm and comfortable.
Ann was nesting. She was in the process of converting our house that was
filled with avocado green everything, dated wallpaper, and dark paneling to
a more updated country look. While I worked, she worked. She stripped
wallpaper and hung wallpaper. She stripped paint and painted. She went
to yard sales and bought other people's castaways and turned them into
our treasures. She was able to see potential in the ugliest chair or stool and
with a little love it became a thing of beauty. Perhaps that's what she saw
in me that one magical night back in the bar, I thought; what I couldn't see
in myself, Ann could.

By early spring, the snow had melted and life began to return to the
ground on which we walked. Ann's pain in her left shoulder followed her
all winter long. At first, it seemed innocent enough. The doctor thought so
too and continued to treat it as bursitis, but the pain didn't go away. They

gave her steroid shots, it still didn't go away. They gave her anti-inflamma-
tory drugs that offered only temporary relief. I saw in her face that something wasn't right. I saw her rubbing her shoulder because the pain just
wouldn't go away.

"Annie, when do you go back to the doctor?"

"I think it's in a couple of weeks, why?"

"It still hurts; I can tell it still hurts."

"Yes, the doctor still thinks all this work I've been doing set off the
bursitis."

"Babe, I am not a doctor, but I really think you should get a second
opinion. I just don't believe this is bursitis. This has been going on for six
months now! Bursitis should go away after a while."

"Oh, John, you worry too much. The doctor said it's nothing to worry
about. Should I call you Dr. John?"

*Ann had been in denial and
I wondered if the doctor
was too.*

"Call me what you want, I am
worried about you."

"I'll be fine, I'll look at the calendar and see when my appointment
is. Maybe I can move it up; will that
make you happy?"

"Your being healthy will make
me happy."

We really liked Michigan and
the small community in which we lived. We made some new friends and
we now only lived a few hundred miles around Lake Erie from Joyce and
Arnie. The climate was more of what we grew up with; we had four seasons
again. I was doing a better job of balancing my career and my life. All was
well except this nagging pain in Ann's left shoulder. She was right about
one thing, I worried too much.

Ann had been in denial and I wondered if the doctor was too. Some
nights I felt her sneak out of bed and attempt to find more comfort on the
couch, in the warmth of her living room. If only the pain would give her
one night off. It went from a dull ache a few months ago to an excruciating
stab. Painkillers were now barely making a dent. Two steroid shots only
took away the pain for a few days. This was not bursitis. I knew it and so
did she.

By June, the pain in her shoulder was worse and now she had a pain in her chest too. There was no racing heart or sweats, just a stabbing pain that lasted a few minutes and disappeared. I was nervous. She had a checkup with the doctor on Monday, June 12 for her shoulder and I urged her to move the appointment up. But once Ann had her mind set on something there was no changing it.

On Sunday, June 11, I had a meeting with an important customer who loved to golf. I left the house filled with worry knowing full well I wouldn't be able to concentrate. I'm bad enough without being preoccupied with other matters and this seemed to me like no ordinary matter. I thought of canceling, given her condition, but she urged me to go. It was a gloomy day in more ways than one and the kind of day when the wind goes through you, chilling every bone in your body.

The plan was for me to meet Ann and the boys at the soccer field after my golf game. It was Eric's last game of the year and if they won the game, they were division champs for the second straight year. Eric was a skillful and determined soccer player. Like his dad, he hated to lose and did almost anything to earn a win for his team. He was not all flash and glory, but hard work and guts. Eric was a coach's dream who showed up every game and every practice ready to play.

This day, though, was different. Eric, like Ann, had not felt well that day and had a fever the day before. Eric was seldom sick, but on the day of the most important game of the year he felt too sick to play. But Eric, being the team player that he was, wanted to attend the game to support the team on to victory.

After my golf date, I raced off to the field to catch as much of the game as possible. I looked around for Ann's car but didn't see it. The field was in a valley and from my car I could see the soccer players but not the boys or my wife. I called home, no answer. Where could they be? Were they at the hospital? Where were the boys? Why was I thinking this way? She had only a little pain in her shoulder. It would go away. Why was I so worried?

Needless to say, without any sign of them at the field, I raced in my car again, this time for home. The ride was twenty minutes but seemed like far longer. I arrived and was relieved to find no note, but no family either. I figured that they must have gone to the game after all and we must have passed each other on the way. If I was right they would be returning home in about thirty minutes.

Thankfully I was right. They walked in the door and Eric had a big smile on his face. His team had won and they were champions again.

"Where were you guys?" I asked.

"We were at the game, Dad. Where were you?" replied a puzzled Eric.

Now I felt horrible that I didn't make my son's last game and indeed the championship game. Eric had always been proud of his athletic accomplishments and though he didn't play, I know he wanted me there.

"I couldn't see your mom's car, so I thought I must have been too late, and I came home. I'm sorry I missed the game, Eric."

Ann was cold and feeling tired and said she wanted to lie down and rest. I knew something was wrong. In all the years I've known Ann, she had never complained of being tired in the middle of the day and never took a nap. Ann was always full of energy, never sitting still for a minute.

As she began walking upstairs, I reached for her arm.

"Are you okay?"

"I'm just a little tired; I didn't sleep well last night. Give me a few minutes to lie down."

I didn't want to press, I had done enough of that, but she hadn't slept well in months. Why, all of sudden, was she so tired now?

She rested for about thirty minutes and returned saying she felt better. She didn't look better. She said she felt well enough to prepare some dinner. I think she thought that would divert her mind away from what was racing through it.

"Is there anything I can do, Ann?"

"You can hug me and keep me warm." Her arms locked around my back, instinctively I did the same to her and she rested her head on my shoulder. "I just want to make time stand still John, right here right now, the four of us."

"I wish I could do that. You sound very concerned, Ann. Is there something you want to tell me?"

"No, we'll just have to see what the doctor says tomorrow. I probably have pneumonia or maybe pleurisy. We'll find out soon enough."

So why didn't I go with her on her appointment? I don't have the answer to that; maybe denial, I guess. Pneumonia was no big deal, I thought, and after all, Ann was a nurse, she should know these things, right? Pleurisy sounded worse, but not much worse and my mind was in a good place then when it came to the conclusion that it all would be all right.

I came home early on Monday. Denial was wearing off. The boys were still in school, the final lazy days of school when little minds wander away to a field, or to water, or to sleeping and dreaming. Life was returning to the land. The sun's rays cascaded though the fresh green leaves and an innocent breeze felt good against a warm face. As I pulled in the driveway, I saw Ann walking over from her friend's house next door. At least three people knew what the doctor had said and denial to this point had kept me from being one of them. I pulled in the garage, shut down the engine, stepped out of the car, and there she was looking at me, her eyes blinking back tears. I hoped they were tears of joy. As I closed the door of the car she took my hands and as she did I prayed that she was about to tell me everything was all right.

It wasn't.

"John, I'm scared. Um, the doctor told me I have fluid in my left lung. That's what's causing this pain in my chest. She doesn't know what's caus-ing the fluid." Ann paused to compose herself, her lip quivering, and she was now crying. "Ummm . . . it could be an infection or it could be cancer. She doesn't know yet and has ordered a CT scan and blood work. She is trying to rule out lymphoma."

I wrapped my arms around Ann and we gently rocked back and forth in the same spot in the garage for several minutes, her tears pouring out on my shoulder and down the back of my shirt. Was this a bad dream?

"John, I didn't believe she was talking to me when she said 'lymphoma.' I'd heard that word said to patients before but when she said it to me I was stunned. I thought for sure I had pneumonia or pleurisy, but lymphoma?"

I was trying to be sensitive. It was all coming at me so fast I couldn't think straight, and as for Ann, she had trouble thinking at all. "I'm sorry I wasn't with you, Annie. I should have gone, forgive me. I won't do that again."

"I wish you were there too. I drove home and could barely see through my tears. I kept thinking about the boys. They're so little, John, and the thought of me being sick scared me."

We stopped rocking and started walking slowly inside to the kitchen and the warmth and comfort of our home. The place that Ann brought alive with her talent to decorate. I pulled up a chair at the table. To my surprise, Ann wanted to sit on my lap. She wanted to be close to me and me to her. I could feel the tremors of nerves running wild through her body.

A storm was brewing . . . a storm that could sweep us off our feet and take us to places we didn't want to go.

"When is the scan?"

"Friday, and I want you to take me." She looked at me, her eyes still filled, waiting for my approving nod. "Then Monday, she'll review the results with us. Tell me I'm all right, John. I just want someone to tell me I don't have cancer."

I put my head into Ann's bosom and never answered her. How could I? What would I have said? We talked a while longer and rationalized about the news. It couldn't be, we thought. There must be some big mistake. Surely someone would tell us it was.

The week dragged on. A torturous grind it was. Life was suddenly out of focus, our world slightly off center. Walking was never more difficult, some things impossible. We knew nothing for sure, but we knew everything, and what we seemed to know was that a storm was brewing, a storm that could erode this cozy beach of ours with the white sand and the lazy breezes. A storm that could sweep us off our feet and take us to places we didn't want to go.

On Sunday night, the night before we would know our fate, Ann and I went to bed early as if trying to hasten Monday's arrival. The days were now growing in length and the last vestiges of the day's sun flickered in through the drawn shades, creating a misty glow to the room.

"John, are you nervous about tomorrow?"

"Yes."

"What are you nervous about?"

"That she is going to tell us something we don't want to hear. I want this be to be some big mistake, but I fear it's not. I woke up this morning and hoped I was dreaming all of this. Reality set in and I wanted to go back to sleep, try it again."

"I did the same thing and I'm nervous about the same thing. I can't believe I might have cancer. This can't be happening, can it?"

I rolled over closer to Ann, encasing her body in mine. I could not get near enough to her as I wanted to feel her heart beat against my skin. I wanted to feel her blood pumping through her veins and to breathe the air that left her lungs.

"Ann, I don't know what is going to happen tomorrow but I do know you mean everything to me and I don't know what I would do without you, so we have to get you well."

"I like hearing that. As long as I'm sick, if I'm sick, keep telling me that."

We snuggled until we slept and while we slept, two peas we were. Darkness fell over us, dreams awaited us, and the morning would come too soon.

In the morning the most beautiful day greeted us: blue skies, sunshine, and mild temperatures. The kind of day when doing nothing at all sounded good. The kind of day when the world around us felt perfect and having not a care in the world would have blended in well with this day.

But this day was to be nothing like that.

Upon arrival in the waiting room, I paced while Ann sat calmly and skimmed through a magazine, never taking more than a few seconds on each page. The waiting room was small and despite the sunshine, seemed gloomy inside, but based on my current state of mind, I couldn't tell if that was real or imagined. It wasn't a long wait, only a couple of trips to the men's room, and then we were invited into a very small exam room that felt even darker than the waiting room, despite the bright fluorescent lights. Along the way, we crossed paths with the doctor and she gave us an affable smile. And if only for a moment I felt a reprieve and my inner dialogue raced to an abstract thought, infection; Ann was all right!

We were sitting for just a few minutes when there was a muted knock on the door and we watched it open and the doctor come in behind it. It seemed like everything was happening in slow motion. Her walk, the blink in her eyes, the hand gestures did not seem in real time and the friendly smile we saw in the hallway had faded away and she was now more businesslike. She sat down on a stool and reached for Ann's hand. A gentle smile graced her face and I knew that was bad.

"Hello, Mrs. O'Shaughnessy. I'm afraid the news I have for you is not good." She paused to compose herself, letting her just-released words sink in. She never took her eyes off Ann. "The scan results were just read to me and they show you have a three-centimeter mass in the upper lobe of your left lung. You also have a pleural effusion and a thickening area which could be malignant."

As the last few words left her vocal cords, Ann melted. I let go of her hand and put my arm around her and pulled her in close to me. Her eyes now crying streams, her feet were pounding the floor in anger, and she screamed out the words, "NO, NO, NO!"

Pausing again, the doctor continued, raising her voice ever so slightly and tried to talk over Ann's emotional outcries.

"We don't yet know what this mass is. We'll need a biopsy to rule out cancer. It could be an infection of some kind. More than likely it's not, but the biopsy will tell us what it is and then we can decide what to do next."

Trying to remain composed while still holding on to Ann, I probed the doctor. "If it is cancer, what type do you think it is?"

"It's probably lymphoma, which is treatable." She paused again and took Ann's hand in hers. Ann never looked up, almost embarrassed to show her face, which by now was a flood. "I'm very sorry to have to give you this news."

"When can she get this biopsy?" I replied. "Can we get it done tomorrow?"

"I doubt that, but if you want I'll make some calls and try to get you in as soon as possible."

"Please do."

Ann and I had just heard words that until now had only been heard by other people. But now, these other people were us.

The doctor looked at Ann knowing there was nothing else she could say that would make any of this more palatable. She rose from her swiveled stool, glancing back at Ann as she exited the room. Blue tissues, wet from Ann's tears, had fallen from her lap onto the tiled floor. Her pants had patches of moisture. Her face remained in a tucked position with her chin touching her neck. I rubbed her back, gentle swipes I made. Words were only words right now and even if I could have said something, I'm not sure she would have heard it.

Ann and I had just heard words that until now had only been heard by other people. But now, these other people were us. It felt like she was caught in the crosshairs of some mad gunman, pressing his aim, locking her in, waiting for the right moment to pull the trigger.

Eric, I'm not sure what you will be when you grow up, I think you will want to draw or write. Collin, you are so young and you can't know what you want to do. Collin, one time this spring while riding your bike you said you were, "kind of nervous about college." I want you boys to be all that you are capable of being. You are both smart boys who can excel in life if you work hard and stay focused. If you want a place by a lake with a wave runner, you could get it, but it will take focus and staying away from drugs and always talking your concerns over with Dad. He will always love you like I do.

A Mother's Journal
August 1995
Ann O'Shaughnessy

11 | A Blade of Grass

*The world around us continued about its business. We felt like a
blade of grass, insignificant, blending into a sea of green, unnoticed
by anyone except God.*

A week later, we found ourselves in a surgeon's office admiring all of
his diplomas and awards brazenly framed on the walls. Despite
feelings that ran the spectrum, in the week in between then and
now we managed each day to put one foot in front of the other and to get
through another sunrise and sunset.

Then we woke up and the nightmare began all over again. We couldn't
shake what we found ourselves in.

After a brief introduction the doctor minced no words and gave us a
copy of the CT scan. It read as follows:

1) *3.0 cm mass within the left upper lobe abuts the mediastinum and there
   is evidence of a possible adjacent infiltration on the mediastinal fat.*
2) *Abnormal soft tissue densities particularly in the carinal region compat-
   ible with lymphadenopathy.*
3) *A large left-sided pleural effusion with adjacent atelectatic lung.*
4) *Pleural thickening particularly at the left base which may be malignant
   in nature given the findings described above.*

None of that sounded good and he assured us none of it was. I didn't know what half the words meant. Ann knew them all. The only word I needed to know and didn't like to read was the word "malignant."

He put the scans on a backlit screen and tried to show us where the problem was.

"Right there," he pointed with his pen to a spot on the scan and circled it. "You see that? I think this is stage four."

There was nothing soft about his approach. Nothing calming, only dire words that suggested it was over for Ann. Ann reached for my hand and grabbed it firmly, squeezing it in the tightest of grips. She needed something to hold on to so she wouldn't collapse on the floor.

"You know I've been doing a lot of painting lately, are you sure this couldn't be something related to that?"

"I am sure," he replied. "Didn't your doctor go over these results with you?"

"Not in this kind of detail," I sadly replied. "She told us it might be an infection, maybe lymphoma but she never said stage four. We would have remembered that."

It was a simple question:

Why?

"You don't have lymphoma. You have a growth in your lung. I believe you have lung cancer. Tomorrow we'll know more."

"Lung cancer? She doesn't smoke."

"It's not as rare as you may think. There is no telling how she may have contracted this. I am truly sorry to have to give you this news."

"What happens tomorrow?" I asked.

"The procedure is fairly routine, but it is major surgery and I'm not saying it won't be without risk. It should take about three to four hours of surgery and then several days of recovery. I'll know more once I get in there, but looking at the scans, I wish I could be more positive. I want to prepare you for the worst, and we can hope for the best."

We parted ways with the doctor. We walked along long hallways and went silent as a myriad of unspoken words danced through our heads. I was amazed how the world around us remained so normal, unfazed by the news we had just been given. It made me feel insignificant, like a distressed blade of grass blending into a sea of green, unnoticed by anyone except God. No one seemed to observe that we now walked with unsteady, less confident gaits. No one seemed to discern the anguished looks on our faces or how the circles beneath our eyes had become more pronounced. No one noticed how our clothes fit more loosely around our bodies, clothes that only a week ago were a size too small.

As I reached in my pocket for my keys to start the car, my mind kept pulling me back to the same question over and over again. It was a simple question: Why?

I always wanted to be there for you boys. To be a mom who could talk freely to you about sex, drugs, love, and relationships. I wanted to give you correct information and to guide you. One day I will be listening to you from heaven and I will pray that you go to Dad.

A Mother's Journal
August 1995
Ann O'Shaughnessy

The boys from Canton Center Road: Collin,
Steven, Eric, and Dan.

12 | No Permission Needed

"Hi Joyce, its John."

"Well, hi, John, how's Annie?" Joyce said this with trepidation in her voice.

"Joyce, you and Arnie need to come out here tomorrow. Annie is not good, she's very sick. The doctor is quite convinced she has cancer."

"Oh my," she sighed.

"She is in surgery from about noon until four. Can you make it out here by then?"

"We'll be there. We'll leave first thing in the morning."

I didn't know what else to say. They packed their stuff and headed to Michigan.

By now, all signs pointed to cancer. The biopsy determined what type and how advanced it was. It was called staging. In surgical terms it was a major operation and one that was not without potential complications. But the doctor did not anticipate any. The least of Ann's worries was this surgery.

Before we went to the hospital, Ann wanted to talk to God and our priest, Father George. I considered us more spiritual than religious. We both went to Mass regularly, but to say we read the scriptures or followed the Word of God would be a stretch. Ann would often comment that going to church didn't make you a Christian person. Living the way a Christian should live made you a Christian. Caring for people, helping others, being kind, thoughtful, and considerate: those were the characteristics that God wanted in His people.

Father George was the pastor at St. John Neumann in Canton. He was a very friendly man with a powerful build who preferred hugs to handshakes. He turned to greet us right as we walked in the church. It was like he knew we were coming.

"Hi, guys, how are you?" asked Father George.

"Hi, Father. This is my wife, Ann, and I'm John." We shook hands, but I didn't finish my introductions before Ann broke down and began weeping.

"Hey, what's all the crying for? What's wrong?"

"Father, today we are on our way to the hospital. Ann is having a biopsy."

Father George leaned over and placed his arms around Ann. He held her close as if to press the disease right out of her body. He pulled away to look into her tear-filled eyes and then hugged her again.

"Can we pray?" he asked.

We walked into his office just inside the church doors. Bookshelves were filled with all the books I expected a Catholic priest to read and some that I wouldn't. His desk was messy; he was dressed casually, in slacks and a gold shirt. I think he planned to golf that day. We gathered in a circle of three. He reached for our hands, held them firmly; we closed our eyes and began to pray.

Our Father, Who art in heaven,
Hallowed be Thy Name.
Thy Kingdom come,
Thy will be done
On earth as it is in heaven.
Give us this day our daily bread,
And forgive us our trespasses

As we forgive those who trespass against us.
And lead us not into temptation
But deliver us from evil.
   Amen.

We continued without interruption.

Hail Mary, full of grace, the Lord is with thee.
Blessed art thou amongst women, and blessed is the fruit of thy womb, Jesus.
Holy Mary, Mother of God, pray for us sinners, now and at the hour of
our death.
   Amen.

Then we concluded, "In the name of the Father, the Son, and the Holy Spirit, Amen."

I felt something while we were praying. I felt connected to God like never before in my life. I felt a presence in that room, a presence which seemed to come over me and in me, engaging me and becoming a part of me, becoming one with me. As I held Ann's hand and listened to us all praying, it was like I heard a voice saying, *You are not alone, I am with you.*

"So tell me, what do they think you have?"

"I have a three-centimeter mass in my lung. They think it's some kind of cancer. This is what we'll find out today. The last week, our lives have been thrown upside down. All I had a week ago was a pain in my shoulder, now this. I have two young boys at home who need me. John needs me; I can't afford to be too sick."

"I am sorry; I will continue to pray for you. May I announce your name during Mass?"

"Yes," said Ann. "That would be nice, the more people I have praying for me, the better. We need all the help we can get right now. We have never needed God more."

"I would like to visit you tomorrow; may I ask where you'll be?"

"Oakwood," Ann replied.

"How long do you expect to be there?"

"Several days, I'm sure."

"I'll stop by. I can't imagine what you are going through right now, but

I will pray for you both and your children. I'll pray that this is some big mistake and later today you'll find out that you are fine."

"I hope you are right, Father," replied Ann.

"God bless you both."

I think we feared that the moment we let go, we would fall into a deep dark hole.

We said goodbye in the form of bear hugs from Father George and we left the warmth of the church—a place where mostly good things could happen, I thought, to a place that was cold and sterile and where bad things could happen and often did.

"Annie, did you feel anything when we prayed?"

"What do you mean?" she asked.

"A presence, did you feel we were not alone in the room?"

"I felt comforted by praying, but I wouldn't describe it as a presence."

"It was like nothing I'd ever felt before."

My mouth cracked just a little at first. I felt my knees go weak and before I collapsed on the cement just outside the church, I dropped to my knees of my own accord. My mouth was now wide open with grief, wrinkles appearing around my eyes with tears squeezing out from beneath my closed eyelids. Ann knelt down next to me and placed her hand on the back of my neck giving me a soft comforting rub.

"Why is this happening to us, Annie? I don't understand! I keep asking myself 'why?' And I never get a good answer back."

"I wish I knew why, John, but I don't. I wish I had answers for the both of us and I wish I had a picture of what the future looked like. But I don't have that either."

"I'm not sure I want to know what the future looks like. That's a picture I'd only want to see if you could paint it for me. And even then, I'd only want to see it if you're in it with me."

Now on the ground, both of us on our knees, we held on to each other and cried aloud. I think we feared that the moment we let go, we would fall into a deep dark hole.

We arrived at the hospital where a cold scalpel awaited Ann, but procedures came first. The hospital had to make sure they'd get paid for all they would do to my wife, the rent for the operating room, the surgeon's fee, the drugs to put her to sleep, and the drugs to keep the pain at bay.

Whether I accepted it or not, it was happening. It didn't need my permission.

We sat behind a computer while a staff worker entered all of Ann's vital information, like where she lived, phone numbers, date of birth, social security number, and, most importantly, why she was here. She signed forms until her hand cramped.

We escaped from the procedures room and began our long lonely walk to the operating room where that cold scalpel was getting sterilized and everything else needed to accomplish this dreadful operation was being prepared. I imagined the surgeon was looking at that scan again and the circle his pen made, "right there," he had said. "Right there."

The walk ended but the journey was just beginning.

"Ann, I don't have any idea how we got here, but I want you to know how much I love you. No matter what awaits us, I'll be with you, we'll do this together."

She looked up at me, her eyes dancing and flicking back tears. "I'm scared to death, John. Pray for me."

"I will Ann, but one more thing. From that first time we met at the Dubliner until this very moment, you have been the center of my life. We were meant to be together, and for reasons we don't understand, we were meant to do this together. And we will do this together, because I can't bear to think of doing anything without you."

She turned her face and rested it on my shoulder and we engaged in a tender embrace. I could feel her tears on my shirt. I did not want to let go and she did not want to leave.

"John, aside from those cheesy poems you gave me when you proposed to me, that's the sweetest thing I think you have ever said, and those words could not have come at a better time."

For two hours I walked the hallways back and forth, the stairwells up and down. I walked outside and came back in. I walked inside and went back out. I visited the men's room often, even when I had nothing to do there. I sat in the waiting room and observed other people who seemed far less anxious than I was and I could only imagine that the reasons they were here were far less critical than the reason I was.

Ann never left my mind. I glimpsed the future and refused to see one without her. I refused to see me without my wife and our sons without their mother. I refused to accept what was happening to us, but it was. Whether I accepted it or not, it was happening. It didn't need my permission.

Four hours into surgery, Joyce and Arnie came walking down the hallway. My eyes welled and then blurred as I ran to them hugging them in the hallway.

"I'm glad you guys are here. I'm a mess and she hasn't even come out yet. She should be finished any time now, I think you got here just in time."

They did. We were not in the waiting room but a few minutes when I turned around and heard the metal doors to the recovery room swing open as it had many times in the last few hours. But this time I looked up and through all the haze in my eyes, I saw Ann's surgeon. He was still in his blue scrubs and blue hat; his eyes fixed on mine and motioned for me to step into the hallway. Joyce and Arnie followed me like wounded dogs.

He wasted no time.

"It's cancer and it's bad. Her lung is filled with it. There is a tumor the size of a tennis ball, it looks like mesothelioma but I can't tell for sure. The biopsy will determine that." He reached for my elbow and said, "I'm sorry."

I replied weakly, "Well, what happens now? Can you take it out?"

"No, I am afraid it's too advanced. She will need chemotherapy, but I'm not an oncologist."

"Is it terminal?"

"I cannot answer that. She will get set up with an oncologist and he or she could help you with that question. I am sorry, Mr. O'Shaughnessy, but I need to go."

I put my back up against the waiting room wall and watched as he went back through the swinging doors and into the recovery room where Ann lay sleeping unaware still that she had advanced lung cancer. I slithered my body down to the cold tile floor and squatted against the wall. I put my hands over my face and went numb. Joyce and Arnie hovered above me crying, but I couldn't help them, I couldn't help myself. After a while, I lost feeling in my legs so I then sat on the floor extending my legs straight out. About that same time, the numbness wore off and the two words "it's cancer" kept repeating in my mind. Tears fell hard from my eyes and there was no stopping them. I put my hands back over my face as if trying to stop the flood coming from my eyes. It was to no avail. They kept coming.

Eventually, we were asked to find refuge in a chapel room not much bigger than a confessional, where the three of us could wail away as loud as we wanted and no one would hear us. It was a circle of tears. When I cried, Joyce cried, when Joyce cried, Arnie cried. For hours we all cried with barely one complete sentence spoken between any of us.

There was no escaping it now. Ann had cancer. It was not an infection, it wasn't even lymphoma. It was the worst of them all, lung cancer. She had a "cancer ball" in her body that was black and I imagined ugly. And I wondered, how did it get there?

I walked out of the chapel room, my eyes rose-red but dry, and through the operating room doors to see her. I didn't know what to say. She was just waking up. The lights were bright and the room was warm like an incubator. The nurses spotted me and seemed to know who I was looking for. Her surgeon talked about tonight's game, made a bluff bet with a male nurse. She lay there all quiet on the gurney. Milk-colored blankets draped around her, needles stuck in her arms; monitors beeped; she turned her head slightly and saw me coming. As I approached her my tears returned. I took her hand in mine; it was warm like the room.

"How's my girl?"

"You tell me."

"Annie, it's cancer." She looked at me, still groggy, but was not surprised. "I'm here for you and we are going fight this thing together, just like I said we would. I love you."

A wry smile was all the emotion that came from Ann. I stayed with her. I was careful not to disrupt the needles that pierced her veins. With my feet on the floor, my head rested uncomfortably on her chest. She gently caressed my hair.

I loved being a stay-at-home mom for you boys. I just loved being your mom, making your beds, cleaning up after you, and seeing all of your school papers. You loved my chocolate chip cookies. You both used to say "give me a taste" and you would lick the spoon filled with raw cookie dough. We loved the mornings. We had about twenty minutes of "snuggle" time. When you finally came downstairs, you would give me a big hug and say, "Good morning, Mom." I loved each hug.

A Mother's Journal
August 1995
Ann O'Shaughnessy

13 | FEEL THE PAIN

I learned that crying felt good. It was only for a moment or two, but eventually those moments added up to an hour, and then a day. The slow release of tears meant I was feeling this pain and not running away from it. Crying is all part of the natural progression of grief.

I dragged myself home that day; tears cascaded down my face. I needed wiper blades on my eyelids, not to be blind. It felt like a big boulder was perched on my back weighing me down and it was only through instincts as old as dust that I was able to stand upright at all.

Joyce and Arnie made it back. Suitcases, still packed, waited for their attention in the kitchen. Our guest room would become their home.

I moved slowly up the stairs, finding my way into the bedroom where I closed the door behind me, keeping the world out. I fell to the bed, face down, assuming the position of a murder victim, chalk lines drawn, motionless. Crying sounds now muffled by the soiled quilt beneath my face. The same quilt Ann made for us to keep us warm and safe when we were at the mercy of God and the night.

After a while of lying stock-still dead, like a branch on the ground, my mind said *move* but my body didn't move. My mind said *turn over* but I remained frozen. My mind said *the boys need me* and it was only then . . .

I moved my big toe first, then my knee bent, and then the other and I turned over and went fetal. Curled up like a baby. *The boys need me* I heard again. *Get up!* My mind was trying to pull me out of bed, begging and pleading with my inert body. *The boys need me.* I finally got up.

I moved slowly to the bathroom. Putting my hands on the sink and locking my elbows in place, I looked in the mirror at someone other than me. Someone who looked haggard, like he had been chased all night by a wild boar, barely escaping the animal's ravenous bite. It was only after I moved in closer that I saw features that resembled the man I was. The blue, bloodshot eyes, the distinctive chin with the cleft, and the thinning brown hair. This poor man in the mirror was me and I looked like hell.

I threw water on my face trying to erase the scars born from an insidious disease in my wife's lung. It was late afternoon, but I thought maybe a shower would do more good, so I stripped down, throwing my clothes to the floor, and stood in a hot shower, banging the palm of my hand against the shower walls. Tears mixing in with piped water, I stood there naked and pitiful, feeling no better than before.

Still those words haunted me: *The boys need me.*

My cries those early months stretched from dusk till dawn.

I dressed and retrieved them from a friend's house. I silently thanked God for these friends, Sharon and John. They're saints, canonize them now. Without friends like them, a long walk off a short plank may have been an easier way out. Once we got back home, I sat the boys down in the living room. Now what? They looked at me, their dad, their eyes as innocent as puppies', and here I was looking like I'd gone the distance between the ropes. A fight I didn't train for and didn't win. Now what? What do I say to them? How do I tell them their mom is dying? That time is running out for her? How in the world do I do this? Someone help me!

Still they looked at me, wanting me to say something, anything. I stammered and stuttered trying to find words that seven- and nine-year-olds could grasp. I wanted to climb back upstairs, crawl back into bed, and resume the same fetal position I had assumed before I heard the words *the boys need me.*

And they did. Now more than ever they needed me and I needed them, too. This was the first glimpse of what life would be like, just the three of us. It scared the crap out me that I was thinking it, and that it might actually happen.

My cries those early months stretched from dusk till dawn. I allowed myself to feel this pain. I felt it deep in my soul. All of this pain, the chaos of it all, the morbid conclusions being drawn so early in the fight. More pain brought more tears. More conclusions, more hurt, throbbing from my toes up my spine, each day much the same.

14 | GRIEF IS LIKE YOUR SHADOW

Grief is like your shadow, you cannot run from it, you cannot hide from it, it's always there: it's just that certain conditions make it clear for all to see.

Grief doesn't start when you lose someone. It is the emotional effect caused by a thought.

Ann recovered in the hospital for the next seven days. I visited often. I was the sales manager at the Sealy mattress plant which was located just fifteen minutes away. I visited each day at lunchtime and on my way home and then again at night. Blood drained from her lung; I was hopeful that the cancer was draining too. It wasn't.

I was told by a social worker that I had post-traumatic stress, a form of grief when your mind basically shuts down when it is temporarily absorbed with anger, despair, and self-pity. Ann's way of coping wasn't by choice, it was morphine.

In the quiet of her hospital room, my head gently rested on her chest and I listened to her heart beat as it thumped away, sounding strong.

"John, I've lived a good life. I was a wife and a mother, that's all I ever wanted to be."

"But, Ann you're so young. Don't give up on yourself and be leaving me so soon. Quit talking in past tense to me, please."

"I'm not, John, but let's face it, it doesn't look real good. I have to deal with reality. I have to face what's going to happen one day or another. You and the boys will be fine without me. You're a good father."

"Why couldn't it have been me? They need you, I need you. I wish it was me that was dying."

"It might have been easier that way. I am more patient than you, but it's not that way. You need to be strong for me and the boys."

"Ah, strength. I remember I had that once, a long time ago. Back then I didn't cry through my shoes like I do now."

My tears fell on her old nightgown. Grief consumed my body. She stroked my hair and was sad, too, but the medicine was helping her. I think the medicine was helping her say things she didn't really mean. I know she began to think about all the things she would probably never witness: watching the boys graduate from high school, seeing them off to college, being walked down the aisle at their weddings, having grandchildren to spoil, and growing old.

You see, every day, Ann was the rock that all of her boys latched onto. She did things for all of us, made sure we were on task. We all counted on that, and Eric and Collin didn't know anything different. She spoiled them, really, and she knew it. As for me, I saw that rock being gone one day, and wondered what I would hold onto.

We changed hospitals from Oakwood to the University of Michigan Medical Center in Ann Arbor. Not only was it closer to our home, it was a world-renowned cancer center and we felt it offered Ann the best opportunity for treatment. It was July 2, and while many people throughout Michigan were preparing for boating and cookouts, Ann was preparing for chemotherapy treatments.

As promised, I didn't miss another important visit.

"Ann, do you mind if I ask the doctor some questions?"

"What kind of questions?"

"Tough questions, things that I would like to know. But I only want to ask if you give me your permission."

"Well, you'd better ask, because I can't."

"But you don't mind if I ask?"

"No."

As we turned the corner, we could see the medical center. It looked impressive but impersonal, a fortress of white cement and windows that blended with the skyline on this cloudy damp day. We passed the emergency room where an ambulance had pulled in and we entered the huge parking garage adjacent to the hospital. The gate opened and the electronic machine asked me to please take the ticket. The garage was dark and dirty and smelled of fumes. We walked past many waiting rooms; they all looked the same—uncomfortable chairs, televisions hung from walls tuned to channels that had no consensus, large clocks that reminded everyone how long they had been there, and magazines carelessly strewn. I was already pacing, the coffee I had consumed all morning was now looking for an escape from my nervous bladder. Just like before, Ann seemed far more relaxed than me. We arrived at our final destination, the waiting room; the television had a game show on. We checked in. I was thankful the bathroom was just a few steps away.

The bathroom became my shelter in the hospital, a little room where I could go if only for a few minutes to catch my breath and pretend that none of this was happening. But it was, and as soon as the latch to door clicked, I stepped back into the real world.

I thought the hospital reeked of dying. I saw sadness on every face. Bald heads with skinny torsos on parade. People whose bodies had let them down and now they were being injected with poisons with names they couldn't pronounce. Ann glanced at the same people; she saw her future and began to cry.

I visited the men's room several times before someone called, "Mrs. O'Shaughnessy" and a nurse ushered us back to the exam room. We passed through more corridors, only now they were much narrower. Barely two people could pass each other without rubbing shoulders. Charts put in bins hung from the walls outside each room making the fit even tighter. We sat down, the door was closed. I heard mumbling in the room next to us. It was our doctor looking over Ann's chart. Soon enough the door opened again.

"Hello, Mrs. O'Shaughnessy."

"Hello, Doctor. I'm John and this is my wife, Ann."

"Are you here for a second opinion?" he asked.

"No, not at all, we understand the diagnosis; we just hope to be treated here at the university."

Seated next to me, Ann just listened. Outwardly she remained calm.

"Well, I have read your scans. I have also reviewed the biopsy report and I believe you have stage 3b lung cancer. It's adnocarcinoma. The good news about this cancer is that it's typically slow-growing. The bad news is it's difficult to stop. You are young and relatively strong so I am going to suggest a very aggressive protocol of two types of chemo agents. You will come here every week for one and the other you will get every six to eight weeks. They are very powerful and we can only hope that they help."

"Can you tell us about them?"

"One is Navelbine and the other Cisplatin. Both have shown promise in treating lung cancer. There will be side effects that we will have to monitor."

"Will I lose my hair?" asked Ann.

"You might."

He looked at Ann the whole time, as if I weren't there. I was thankful for that; she was his patient. He gave us all the time we needed.

"What exactly does 'help' mean?" I asked.

"Well, we are looking for a response to the drugs, meaning the tumor is shrinking. We hope to reduce its size by about thirty to forty percent. That would be successful."

"Why can't you operate and take it out?"

I was walking a tightrope, with one eye on the present and one eye on the future, trying to balance on today.

"I could show you the scan, but the tumor has invaded her diaphragm. We believe the best protocol is chemo first and then maybe surgery, depending on how successful we are with chemotherapy."

I don't know where I got the strength to ask this next question. Something came over me and I wanted to know the unknown and I wanted him to tell me now.

"I can see you are not thinking about a cure here, so how long would we have if you get a response?"

"Very, very difficult to say and I hesitate to tell you, but I would say given her overall health, probably twelve months, maybe eighteen. We will do our very best. If this agrees with you, we can get started on the sixth."

Ann was expressionless. The clock was ticking.

"I'll see you on the sixth."

The reality was I expected to be planning a funeral in three to four months. A year sounded so much better; stretch that maybe to eighteen months. And as sad as that was, Ann was dying and there was nothing I could do about that. But I was walking a tightrope, with one eye on the present and one eye on the future, trying to balance on today. Teetering and leaning, not wanting to fall into some dark abyss.

Make It Go Away

Life as we knew it changed forever and a day
The morning sun that never came became a day painted gray.
But don't despair, there'll be more time
You have so much more to give
Make it go away, this pain you feel
You have so much more to live
Make it go away
Far from here
To a place
Where no one is near,
Make it go away
In a blue balloon
Fill it with air
Right to the moon
Make it go away
Do it for me and your little man
Do it for you
Do it with all you can
Make it go away for the ones you love
For they love you
They want to see you well
To pull you through
You must find the inner strength
And I will help you each and every day
To dissolve this thing within
To make it go away
Be an inspiration for the ones who will follow
Make it easy for them to say
She had these things she never wanted
And she made it go away.

With love, your husband and friend. June 1995

15 | THE THINGS THAT MATTERED MOST

The lens that I looked at life through was quickly refocused.
I once chased money with a vengeance and now I learned
I was chasing a ghost.

We lived in a small community and word spread quickly, like rumors on a thousand tongues, of Ann's illness. People talked about her being the young mother with two small sons and a young husband. She had lung cancer. No one knew how she got it. It was incurable, inoperable, and she was dying. She was getting chemotherapy treatments that would hopefully slow the progression of the disease, but these treatments made her weak and sick. She needed help.

Our world was spinning on an axis we were unfamiliar with. We were fighting an opponent we couldn't see, couldn't touch, couldn't negotiate with, and didn't understand. It outnumbered us. It lived off Ann's blood supply and was multiplying twenty-four hours a day. Our strategy was to poison the well. This would not defeat the enemy, but maybe it would slow it down. I likened cancer to a suicide bomber: when the patient dies, the cancer dies, its job completed.

One morning, not long after the madness began, I opened the newspaper and my eyes were drawn to a headline.

Researchers Find Gene Therapy Effective Against Lung Cancer

The article went on to say doctors were adding years to the lives of people with inoperable lung cancer, the nation's deadliest and most common type of cancer. The therapy destroyed or shrank tumors in six of nine patients. It was an important milestone in cancer research. Chemotherapy was extending people's lives from one year to two years and a new type of radiation available in Detroit was showing more promise. It was called neutron radiation. It had four times the killing capacity as conventional radiation. I read this article and felt hopeful. I thought maybe Ann's death sentence was about to get a reprieve.

The rides Ann made to get her weekly treatments were peaceful enough, if not what was waiting for her. She found a back road that took her by her favorite country store where she could look for a knick-knack or two that would add to our home. Inevitably, whatever she purchased was green. I delighted every time she brought something home, because every time she did, she smiled.

Navelbine was very mild in comparison to Cisplat. I wrongly gauged the effectiveness of the treatments by the heaving she did afterward. If cancer in Ann's body was a forest fire, I pictured the Cisplat as a monsoon rainstorm.

By early September, school was resuming. The air was still hot and sticky but the cool breezes weren't far away now. I went to see Ann at the hospital after her second Cisplat treatment, and hoped to take her home with me. I entered her double-occupancy room and noticed she was all alone. She was in the first bed and the curtains were open, allowing the morning sun to brighten the room. I leaned over her bed and placed a kiss on her forehead.

"Good morning, how do you feel?"

"Like I look, terrible. I was up most of the night sick. I had dreams that were horrifying; bugs were crawling all over me. I want to go home today, I miss the boys. They need their mom, John."

"I know they do, and I need you too, you know. Do you need anything?"

"Ice chips would be nice, my mouth is dry."

"Let me get them for you, Ann." The ice machine was just across the hall at the nurses' station. Gathering ice gave me time to gather my thoughts. I said hello to the nurses who said hello back, not knowing my name.

I placed the large cup of ice chips on her hospital table that swiveled across her bed, and then dragged a chair across the floor, moving it in closer to her.

"John, how did I get into this mess? I mean I'm dying, I can't believe I'm dying. I'm not even forty years old and I'm dying."

I sat in the chair, looked into her eyes, and reached for her hand. I reached for something to say and could think of nothing, nothing that could take her pain away. I was stuck, at a loss for the right thing to say.

"Is he letting you go home today?"

"I don't know. I hope so. He'll come by this morning and let me know. I can be just as sick at home as I am here. But at home I can hug my boys. That's the best medicine right now."

We sat and talked for hours that day, waiting for the doctor to come by and discharge her. Ann wanted to talk some more, I wanted to push a switch and rewind the last few months. I wanted to go back in time and plead with Ann to have someone take another look at that shoulder of hers. Beg and plead, and even cry if I had to. Stomp my feet and say, "God damn it, something is wrong with you, don't you know that? You don't have a shoulder act like that unless something is wrong with you!" Maybe I would have shaken her if I had to and marched her into another doctor's office, a doctor who actually knew the difference between bursitis and cancer. I did none of that, but wished I had done more. If I had, maybe, just maybe none of this would have been happening to my wife.

But it was. The rewind switch didn't work.

Ann got to go home that day. Her tender, loving, innocent pumpkins waited for her back home. But going home was never easy either.

"John, you've got to pull over."

"Here, on the side of the road?"

"Pull over."

I slowed the car down and pulled to a stop on the side of the road, just beyond her favorite store. Ann got out quickly, walked a few feet off the road, and with her hands on her knees, threw up in the grass.

"Now, take me home."

The summer finally faded. Ann continued her weekly rides to the hospital where the poisons awaited her. Fall had been our favorite season; it was the season we met. It was then that we had more innocence and joy. It was then we knew we didn't have much, but everything we needed was everything we had in each other. What we didn't know was that we hadn't lived yet. She traveled the same streets past the same store; only now, dead leaves covered her path. As beautiful as autumn was, it was the season of transformation. What was alive just a few months ago was now dead or dying.

In the first six months of treatment, Ann received thirty courses of chemo, but the cancer still grew. Twice she had to be taken to the hospital for an irregular heartbeat as the tumor's tentacles had invaded the lining of her heart. The treatments were not working.

I went to the library to learn and it offered me a brief distraction from what waited for me at home. I wanted to know everything about the enemy my wife was battling. I went online to investigate clinical trials and cutting-edge research that would cure people of this disease. I became familiar with some of the drugs she was taking; Cisplatin, Navelbine, Compozine, Neupogen, the list became very long. Anti-nausea drugs like Compozine gave her bad dreams. Neupogen filled her with enough white blood cells so she could be injected with more poison. It was a vicious cycle.

By Thanksgiving, we finally got some good news. It seemed the tumor's insidious hold on Ann's heart wasn't as strong as we feared. For now, it retreated and assumed a watchful position, waiting for another opportunity to strike. It slithered in the darkness of Ann's lung, only slightly wounded, as if it was teasing us. Round one was our victory. It was Ann's victory, but the fight was only beginning. We went back to Darien, back to the country, back to peace, and for a few short days we celebrated.

Just before Christmas, I got a raise. My raises were now bigger than my salary when I met Ann. I smiled for a second then felt empty. My company was sold and I had some stock options that were cashed out. Many of my friends received similar checks. Some bought boats and fancy cars with their newfound wealth, and I held nothing against them. Maybe it's what I would have done. I still felt empty.

And so it was, 1995 had finally, mercifully come to an end. It ended the way it began, quietly.

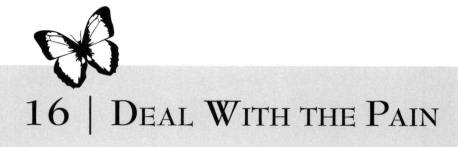

16 | DEAL WITH THE PAIN

I fought off acceptance as long as I could, all the while
feeling sorry for myself, Ann, and the boys. Then I realized
this disease didn't care how I felt. Time was wasting; I needed to
deal with this thing.

S can days were dreadful. It was on those days that we sat in an exam room at the oncology center and listened to Ann's doctor give us an update on her condition. The walk was always the same. The hospital never changed, many of the people became interchangeable. It was like a play. When we arrived, Ann looked around for the friends she made on her many visits to receive chemotherapy. Oftentimes she looked around and found someone missing. She feared the worst, but hoped she would see them next time. She always smiled when she saw a friend.

I smiled too, but thought, "Good people are dying here."

The aroma in the hospital was always the same. There was nothing natural about this smell and it consumed me; it filled my nostrils for days. I observed hairless heads on withered bodies too weak to walk and pushed around in wheelchairs. Some people were actually getting better, but it was hard to tell who was and who wasn't. They were all here for much the same reason we were. I studied the people; I hoped they didn't feel my icy stare as I contemplated mortality. My mind wondered and I contemplated many things. Where were we in this process? How long did Ann have? What would the end look like? It became too much for me to think about.

Before long, we were taken back to the exam room where we waited again. I assumed my spot on an uncomfortable chair across from the sink; Ann took her spot on the exam table where some fresh paper had just been rolled out. In these positions, we waited tensely but hopefully for some good news.

"Hello, Mrs. O'Shaughnessy. How are you today?"

"Not bad, I guess. How am I doing?" Ann replied in the raspy voice that was a constant reminder of how sick she was.

"No change. That's good. It hasn't grown."

Seldom did the doctor refer to the tumor for what it was. The tumor was always referred to as "it" or "mass," not "tumor" or "cancer." It's just how he did it as if not to give the cancer any respect.

"Has it shrunk any?" I asked.

"The CT scan is not precise, but it still reads a three-centimeter mass. This is good."

Every scan day we had was good. The tumor never got any larger than its original size of three centimeters. It never got any smaller either, but it wasn't the tumor we had to worry about, it was its offspring. The doctor examined Ann. He asked her to breathe in and breathe out. He knocked her knees with a device that looked like a rubber arrowhead. It was good if she kicked. He rubbed her shoulder, shook my hand, and we were free to go home.

A year had now passed and we felt blessed that Ann was still with us. She was forty years old. Gallons of poison had poured through her veins. All things considered, she was doing well. The chemo seemed to be working, but it was never a sure thing to know it was. If you saw her in the grocery checkout line you might think she had just recovered from the flu but never would you think she had cancer running through her body.

Right after Ann turned forty, it was as if she knew she was on borrowed time. She was approaching the eighteen-month mark, the outside timeline that the doctor gave her last year. On the outside, she remained steadfast and upbeat, but on the inside she knew otherwise.

"John, I want my picture taken."

"Okay."

She smiled as the picture was taken and looked as if nothing was wrong. Perhaps nothing was. Perhaps Ann was at peace.

"I want a studio portrait of me. I need to have this done, before my hair starts falling out and I start looking like a cancer patient. I want people to remember me looking good. I want my mother to have this picture of me. I want the boys to look at me one day and see this."

She framed her face with her hands, striking a model's pose.

There was another reason she wanted this picture. When she was being eulogized, ravaged by the disease that took her life, she wanted the hundreds of people who came to pay their respects to remember her for how she once looked: the beautiful thick mane of hair, the adorable and contagious smile, and her pretty eyes.

It was an unusually warm fall day. She wore a red turtleneck underneath a Christmas sweater. The sweater was green and blue. To anyone else watching this, it probably looked odd, but to me, I was watching my brave wife have her picture taken knowing when most people saw this, she would be dead. She smiled as the picture was taken and looked as if nothing was wrong. Perhaps nothing was. Perhaps Ann was at peace.

Christmas was approaching. Eighteen months had arrived without fanfare. At times, for a minute or two, I almost forgot that Ann was sick. The snow had yet to fall. She had just spent the day Christmas shopping. And then I heard a thud and a lump formed in my throat.

"Dad come quick, Mom fell!" Eric yelled.

I was running upstairs before I heard his call. I didn't have far to go, my thirty-nine-year-old legs were taking me as fast as they could go. I grabbed the railing, leaping two steps at a time. Within seconds, I arrived at the source of the thud, and there was Ann banging her head uncontrollably up against the linen closet door. Her legs flopped like fresh catch on dry land.

She made barking sounds and tried to speak, only she couldn't. I put my hand under her neck, pulled her gently away from the closet, looked into her eyes, and received back a blank look. They looked like marbles: cold, dilated, and fixed.

"Eric, can you call 9-1-1? Tell them to hurry."

He never answered me but I heard him talking inaudible words beneath Ann's yelps. It was now a few minutes into her first seizure and she showed no signs of coming out of it. I continued to hold her but could not contain her flailing body. I didn't know what to do but I vaguely remembered her telling me about Arlene's seizures. Something about her tongue, so I kept her mouth open and tried to make sure she didn't bite it or allow it to obstruct her airway.

"Eric, buddy, stay where you are and wait for the ambulance."

"Okay."

After the longest five minutes of my life, Ann started to calm down. I was thankful Collin was at a friend's house. She still stared through me. My heart was bouncing up against my ribs. I just held her in my arms and waited for help. From where I held Ann, I could see the back of Eric's head looking out the window waiting patiently for flashing red lights. He was waiting for someone to help his mom.

I knew from the first moment I saw Ann lying on the floor, her neck bent back against the closet, that this was bad. The three-centimeter mass that we had kept such a watchful eye on for the last eighteen months was alive. It never grew, it just spread, its offspring marching like soldiers, building a new beachhead in her brain.

In a few minutes, helped arrived, Eric did very well. Ann was now more lucid but she was still lying on the floor scared. Her legs were limp. The EMTs decided to fold her in a bed sheet and carry her downstairs. I thought it was odd, but they assured me it was the safest way. They asked for her medical history. I told them she had lung cancer. They knew, like I did, that it was now in her brain.

Outside, the neighbors gathered like bees to honey. Their curiosity was getting the best of them. It was December and they were getting cold, but they wanted to know how they could help.

The sheet method worked and Ann was safely removed from the house. She lay on a gurney and reached for my hand, wanting me to tell her she was going to be all right. She still couldn't speak. I wished I could tell her all would be well. Instead I told her I loved her, that I was sorry any of this was happening. I would see her at the hospital and she would feel better by then.

I always told my boys that they were smart and capable of doing whatever they wanted if they finished college and did their best. They would never disappoint themselves.

A Mother's Journal

August 1995

Ann O'Shaughnessy

17 | ALL THINGS PRETTY

I'll be in all things pretty—the sunset, the sunrise, the gentle waves
against the shoreline, a beautiful bird that catches your eye.
Look for me and you will see me.

O n a lazy summer Sunday morning, I was reading the *Detroit Free Press* and I was drawn to a headline. <u>Pillsbury Slims Down the Doughboy.</u> For maybe the first time in months, I smiled. They finally listened to me, I thought. The article went on to say that America was more health-conscious than ever, trying to slim down and tone up. That being the case, the doughboy needed to do the same. He didn't lose much, they showed a before and after. That wasn't the point; the point was I was right. I was a trendsetter, slightly ahead of the curve.

On our last trip to Florida, the Gulf Coast, Ann and I lay in bed one night, the boys having long since exhausted themselves due to all the sun and water, and we weren't far behind. They loved playing together, those boys did. And we loved watching them.

"John, will you bring the boys back here after I'm gone?"

"I don't know Ann, I haven't really thought about that. Lately, thinking about the future is something I have tried to avoid altogether. I am just glad we have this time with each other right now."

"Well, you know, John, they might be sad if you come back here without me. I just want you to be aware of that. They'll miss me when I'm gone and they'll see me in the places I was."

I turned over in the bed. The room was as black as coal and I felt for the outline of her head, placing my hand on the side of her face.

"Annie, we'll be sad no matter where we are without you. At least if we came back here we would be warm and we could try to remember all the great times we had with you."

"I know, but I just worry about them so and it makes me sad to think that you'll come back here without me. All the things the four of us did, now it will only be three of you, someone will be missing. You'll all look for me and I won't be there. I mean, I don't blame you for wanting to come back here, I just wish I could be here with you."

I'll be in all things pretty—the sunset, the sunrise, the gentle waves against the shoreline, a beautiful bird that catches your eye. Look for me and you will see me.

"Believe me, babe, I wish you could, too. If you prefer we not come here, I won't."

"No, I don't want that either. I don't know what I want. I do want you to be happy. Maybe you can you tell me you're coming here and I can look in on you."

"How will I tell you?"

"Pray to me, John, I will always hear your prayers."

"How will I know it's you?"

"I'll be in all things pretty—the sunset, the sunrise, the gentle waves against the shoreline, a beautiful bird that catches your eye. Look for me and you will see me."

"All things pretty, Annie; I'll be looking for you."

The offspring of that three-centimeter mass in Ann's lung had indeed found their way to her brain. She had three tumors there, but still they were not called tumors, they were called lesions. They couldn't be removed with a scalpel; they had to be destroyed with radiation.

By January 1997, Ann knew what the doctors didn't want to admit. Her life was counting down. She wondered if she had just seen her last Thanksgiving turkey or her last Christmas with her boys. If her life was a book, she was reading the last few chapters and wondering how it would all end.

The cancer had now advanced beyond the containment zone. The protocol was radiation rays pounded into her head every week trying to destroy these tiny nubs of blackness. A different chemo agent was used; Cisplat was replaced by Carboplatin. More fancy words. They all did the same thing, killed cancer cells; only they didn't kill enough of them. The forest fire was reigniting inside her body. Dark embers, dormant for a while, fueled by a mystery, were coming to light.

What has always pleased me is the love and respect they showed for each other. They are close brothers and I hope they always remain close. My heart swells with happiness knowing how loving we all are. It's a peaceful gift.

A Mother's Journal
August 1995
Ann O'Shaughnessy

Collin and Eric in Disney World 1990.

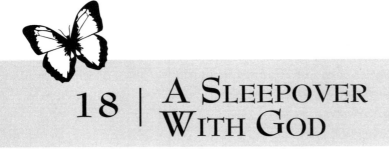

18 | A SLEEPOVER WITH GOD

I know God will only give me what I can handle; I just wish he didn't trust me so much.

Mother Teresa

I think it was Collin who got Ann started on her spiritual journey. He invited God over to sleep in his pop tent. He set it up all by himself in his bedroom. He borrowed his brother's sleeping bag so God would be nice and warm.

"Mom, can I have God over to sleep with me in my tent?"

"Sure, Collin, that would be fine."

"Well, I kind of already checked with Him and He said He was free. He'll be coming real early in the morning."

"Well, what will you do?"

"Oh, I don't know, play video games maybe. But Eric can't stay, there is only room for two. God and me."

The next morning, Ann asked him how it went with God.

"It went great, Mom, He's a lot of fun."

Within forty-eight hours of her seizure, Ann was getting full brain radiation. The doctors assured us that the radiation would be successful. It would kill the lesions. Problem was, it would kill lots of other things, too. The first thing it killed was her hair.

In the quiet of our bathroom, while much of the world was preparing to go sleep, another day done, Ann started pulling her hair out. It came out in clumps, and within minutes her once-thick mane was gone, leveled by a gigantic radiation machine. She shaved the stubborn remains with a disposable razor and flushed it all down the toilet. She looked in the mirror, saw a hairless head, and didn't know whether to laugh or cry. So she did neither. Like everyone else, she went to bed.

Slowly but surely, cancer was stripping things away from Ann. Because of the seizure, she couldn't drive for six months; that meant she'd have to rely on other people to cart her around. She hated that. She lost her sense of taste. Now she couldn't enjoy all those delicious meals that kept coming everyday. Being bald, Ann lost her sense of privacy. People stared at her.

Now she knew her death was looming in the shadows like a serial killer and now it was time to know God.

Everyone who came to know Ann grew to love her. They all saw what I saw in her, a kind, gentle, loving woman who gave to others long before she gave to herself. She always loved God, she prayed regularly, but now she knew her death was looming in the shadows like a serial killer and now it was time to know God. As people grew closer to Ann, she grew closer to God and she felt God was making that happen. I did too. But she felt people were praying for the wrong thing. They were praying for the impossible, she wasn't. She consistently prayed for God to give her time and her family strength and peace. She asked God to watch over her family after she was gone. She didn't ask for her body to be healed. She wanted what Collin had, a sleepover with God. What better way to get to know Him? Other people could be healed by God she thought, I just want to know Him better so when I go to see Him, I'll know what He looks like.

Long before Ann took sick, she had life figured out. It was better to give than receive. Ann was a giver. She knew that the stuff people accumulate in their lives will eventually rust, decay, be stolen, and be voided by a multitude of issues. It gives them temporary peace, but when one gives, it nourishes the soul and the soul, she believed, was forever.

In February, Ann had begun her second month of brain radiation. It was killing everything in its path; even the lesions were dying. She bought some bandanas and began wearing them more often than the wig. I liked that because the wig reminded me that time was running out, that she was sick and dying, the bandanas reminded me that she once had a beautiful head of hair and now she didn't. There weren't many people that could carry a look with a cheap scarf wrapped around their bald heads. Ann could.

When Ann prayed she was specific. She would tell God what she wanted and it was relatively simple messages of peace, strength, and time. I know it was so important for her to see Collin receive his First Communion and I know she prayed for that. She prayed to God to allow her the honor of seeing her son receive His.

How badly she wanted to see her baby's first step unto an altar. When she was first told she was dying, it was almost two years away, and she doubted she would ever get there, but as time drew closer she begged for it to happen. She willed it to happen and in the springtime it did happen.

But still the slippery slope persisted. By early summer the cancerous lesions had found a new home, in her breasts. It was not one small lump; both her breasts looked like they were filled with popcorn. It was as if she woke up one day and there they were. More radiation and the chemo protocol were changed again for second time in four months. They stopped Navelbine and gave her Vinblastin. They also pounded her breasts with more radiation. Her skin turned red and itchy.

And nothing changed. She just got sicker. The doctors knew they were running out of time and drugs to give her. The slippery slope was getting steeper and narrower. By fall, the weather cooled, and it was like Ann's slope was made of ice.

My dear Eric,

I am writing you this letter so you will always have something to hold on to. It's with such sadness and anger that I write this letter. I hope you remember that I always tried to fight the cancer and tried to be brave and strong along the way.

Eric, you were my first born. My real goal in life was to be married, have a home, and be a mother. So simple, yet that is what life is all about. Not the money or material things. My life was always so rich with love. You and Collin were a blessing, the likes I can't describe. I am not sure any mom could have loved their children more than I did you boys.

You were born almost two weeks early on Palm Sunday, very small (6.5 lbs) with dark eyes and hair. People would comment what a beautiful and handsome baby you were. Right from the start you entertained yourself, you were inquisitive and content.

My years with you were so memorable. How you loved the movie Cinderella, as you would watch it over and over. You would say, "Hurry, Mom, here comes the beautiful dress." I was always able to draw cartoon characters but you were so creative and I admired that so. You had so much more talent than your mom.

As a little guy you would wake me almost every night and want me to sleep with you. That is why you got the full-size bed, and I was always glad to crawl into bed at two in the morning with my little man.

As a mom I did so much for you. I'd zipped your coat, picked up your things from the floor. I loved being your mom. I know since I left it's been hard on you and I am so glad I got to do those things all those years.

We shared so much with me staying home. How I loved being a stay-at-home mom. I loved all of our vacations, parties, birthdays, and bedtimes so very much. Trust me, we did tons and had fun.

Eric, you have a great personality. You are well-rounded and have good values and you are well respected by Mom, Dad, Collin, and your teachers. All of your life you were told that and I pray that it continues. I worry about you and Collin's future. I know how hard it will be and I am angry and saddened. Dad and I want you to have a wonderful life filled with all the great things life has to offer—college, family, and happiness. I pray that you will stay away from drugs. I did not participate with drugs when I was in college, and I hope that you will just say "no." There are so many pressures to do things from ages sixteen to twenty-four and I hope you will make good choices. If you do, your future as an adult will be bright. Know I am in heaven watching over you. Always talk to God and ask Him for help in hard times. While I had cancer I always asked God for strength to help me cope with what I was facing so I could continue to be a good mom with the time that I had left.

One of my greatest joys is the way you and Collin treat each other. You are the best of friends, so respectful to each other and always loving. It's how God helps me to know that you will always have each other. Please always be close, family means everything.

I wonder all the time what you will be when you grow up. Whatever your choice is you can do it. You are a smart little boy with so much potential. You used to want to be a fireman, then a dentist and now a soccer player. You always wanted five kids, with some of them having Russian names. Your girl you wanted to be named Crystal. Do you recall this?

How I wished I could be there with you. I hope you will always recall my love. I wonder how I get that message across. I love you all so much and would do anything for you. I did fight the cancer with all I had.

Always know that you can talk to Dad about anything. Dad

was always the impatient one, hot-tempered and sometimes tired. I am sure things will be tough for you as I was always the buffer. <u>Just know that he will always love you and he will be there for you.</u> If you are in pain or trouble, he will always be there for you. Parents are there for their kids.

Eric, I so love you with all of my heart and as I write this letter I hope to live a long time yet, but I want you to have a note to hold on to. It's a powerful message of love. I will see you again one day in heaven. May you have a long healthy life filled with God's goodness. Always treat others well and try to be the person God wants you to be.

I love you,
Mom
January 1997

19 | REALITY

Reality settled over Collin like thick fog. The more he tried
to peek through the more lost he became.

She was twenty-five and I was twenty-four all those years ago back in the Irish pub, back when my worries were on the tip of my nose, easily erased by the smell of chocolate chip cookies or the slightest distraction of anything at all. I worried about gas money and beer money and would I please my boss anytime soon. Back then, at my young age, the age many people find themselves making assumptions about things: assumptions that life will move along just how it was planned and just how it was dreamed. Back then, life hadn't moved me to a place called reality, where hopes are dashed along the rocks and hearts carved up into pieces.

All of 1997 was a blur. Too numerous to count were all my worries. They just blended together with the chaos that ran me ragged. But still I was surviving it all. Waking up each day and taking on a new one, armed with a little more knowledge about what to do and how to feel, I was managing. Managing to get our boys through this, managing to prepare myself and them for the inevitable conclusion of their mother's death.

Ann was preparing the boys and me. As a nurse, she knew what the score was. She was losing, and more importantly, she knew what inning it was and that it was late in the game of her life. Some people knew the score too, and were already walking the ramps heading home. She was writing letters to the boys and me, that at this point I knew nothing about and nor did I want to. She was climbing a mountain, going somewhere we couldn't go, searching for things to leave behind so we'd always remember her.

As if we'd ever forget.

"Boys, your dad and I wanted to talk to you again about Mommy's condition. We both feel it's important for you know how I'm doing, good or bad, so you won't be surprised if something were to happen to me. Have either of you noticed that I seem to be getting sicker?"

We all cried that night. Swept away along the rocks were the faintest of hopes that Ann would ever get well again.

Eric nodded his head. Little Collin just sat there, his legs hanging over the couch a foot off the floor, picking his fingernails and staring back at his mother waiting for her to say something.

"You know I love you boys and your father more than anything. It pains me so that I am so sick and getting worse. The cancer is spreading and it's now in my brain. I don't think the doctors are going to be able to contain it much longer, and at some point, and I don't know when that will be, I am going to die from this disease. You need to know that."

Eric nodded again, indicating to Ann and me he understood all that was said. I'm not sure he even needed those words to be spoken. Without knowing it, I think Eric was one of those people who knew the score and walked the ramps, wanting to go home early and find his mother well again, trying to contain his emotions as best he could and hoping still it was all a bad dream. Collin, it seemed, was not so well-informed. His innocence, his youth had insulated him from the horrors that surrounded him. Some days, I'm not sure he even noticed his mother's hair was gone.

"Mom, you mean you're going to die?" he asked.

"Well Collin, at some point in time we all die. But I'm very sick and I will be dying sooner than I expected. It hurts me so to be telling you those words. I have done the best I can do to this point and I'll continue to fight, but at some point down the road I will lose this fight and I will go be with God in heaven."

Eric rose from the couch first, walked across the room and gave his mother a hug around her neck as if to say what a brave mother he had. Ann wrapped her arms around his small waist. Collin, on the other hand, sat there stunned and started to cry.

"Collin, it's okay, pal, to cry," I said. "You can cry all you want; Daddy has cried enough for all us. Now it's your turn, so let it out."

And he did cry. Reality settled over Collin like thick fog. The more he tried to peek through, the more lost he became. I wrapped my arms around our baby boy and let his tears fall. He kept looking at his mother across the room trying to pretend to be what he was. Ann was crying too, exchanging glances back at him trying to pretend to be what she wasn't. We all cried that night. Swept away along the rocks were the faintest of hopes that Ann would ever get well again.

My dear Collin,

I hope this letter helps you know how very much Mom loved you. It is so hard to write this to my little eight-year-old who I adore, but I need you to know how special you are.

When I think of you I think of my little happy-go-lucky funny guy. You love silliness and love life. You have a heart of gold filled with kindness yet you have a real sensitive side. You can be quiet and hold things in, that's why I worry about you when I die. Talk to Dad and tell him your fears and pain. It's real painful for me to think about leaving you. Dad and I talked about this a lot and we talked to a therapist. My number-one concern was that you and Eric continue to enjoy life and do well. Our time will come again in heaven, hopefully when you're ninety and ready to die. I will be waiting to hold you again. Here in the afterlife is where our answers lie.

My little baby, my last born. You were a pistol in the beginning. A fussy little eight-pound baby as you had so many ear infections. We told you you had broken ears. But despite the constant crying we so loved you. You talked early at eighteen months. Funny now how most people say you are quiet.

As a baby, your number-one person was your brother. How proud I was as a mom to have such loving children. That gives me such comfort to know you will always have each other and with such love. Please remain close as family is number one.

Do you recall that you would never wipe your own butt? Not until six years old. Do you remember in Kansas when you were only three arguing with me over clothes? You hated turtlenecks and I insisted you wear them. We would yell at each other as you were always aware of fashion. Far different from Eric.

You were always a "blankie" boy. We would hide them and say the tooth fairy came and took them away, but you would just

find another and get attached to it. It would always stick and turn gray but you loved it. You would say "blankie" as a boy.

You broke your arm near the elbow at age four by falling out of a wagon. At age seven you broke it again with the babysitter. We kept fixing you up because we loved you. Mom and Dad would do anything for you. Know that you can always talk to Dad even though he can be impatient and sometimes hot-tempered. Keep talking and he'll eventually get it. Mom always worked to balance Dad's moods. Now you kids will have to figure that out. But Dad always will love you and will do anything he can for his boys.

Your godparents, Laureen and Brian, love you too. Talk with her about anything. That's her role now, to play Mom. I am so angry that cancer took me from you. Collin, I adored you. I want you to love life and enjoy all the goodness it has to offer. Say "no" to drugs and make good decisions with your life. Always work hard and you can do anything. You are one smart little boy who can go far. You always said you wanted to do "sales like Daddy."

One thing you always begged for was a dog named "Biscuit." I know someday you will.

As you know, we held you back from starting school at age five. The reason was you were missing the desire to learn. You were home with me and you wanted to play and have fun. Nothing wrong with that, and it has nothing to do with how smart you are. You just were not ready to buckle down and learn. So far, it was the right decision as you are doing well in second grade.

Collin, you are a great little boy, so kind and respectful. Very loving, you give me many hugs. You always bring a smile to my face. My heart is so full of love for you and I hope you can remember that love. Talk to me in heaven, as I am watching you and listening. Right now you have a great love of God, that is wonderful. He is always with us. God gives me strength right now to fight

the cancer and stay strong.

Collin, I loved being your mom. No mom on earth loved their children more than I did. Please remember that you are loved.

Love,
Mom
February 1997

I have always thought of myself as a woman of faith, but not necessarily practicing, going every Sunday, thinking of God every day. But as a nurse I would not let anyone die without those last rites. It was so important to me.

Ann's interview with Mary Mitsch
Summer 1998

Ann and Collin, his first communion.

20 | MAKE A DIFFERENCE IN SOMEONE'S LIFE

The greatest feeling anyone can have is the feeling of amazing joy in knowing they made a difference, however large or small, in someone's life.

When we lived in Kansas, Ann became an entrepreneur. Her business was children's wall hangings. She made up business cards and called her business "Hanging Around." All she needed was her old sewing machine, some scissors, a ruler, and the dining room table. She made three-dimensional works of art made of brightly-colored cloth, felt, soft foam, and lots of love. She took custom orders and also sold her wares through a local consignment shop. Her most popular wall hanging was the mascot for the University of Kansas, the KU Jayhawk, but she made others; Minnie Mouse and Pooh Bear were also popular. She worked several hours a day and sometimes into the night, she and her sewing machine belting out another work of art. She was the only full-time employee but every now and then she'd put her men, big and small, to work picking up scraps or delivering the finished work to its rightful owner. "How much money am I collecting, Ann?" I'd say to her. "Oh, I don't know, I think I told them $20." I'd roll my eyes knowing full well the material cost as much. But the business, much like life, wasn't an exact science for Ann. She did things to put smiles on people's faces, not money in her bank account.

The children's oncology clinic at the hospital in Ann Arbor was adjacent to the adults'. Only a door separated the two. After her treatment, Ann walked through to see the little kids as they received their own treatments. Her heart wept for every sick child. She sat and talked to the children, even volunteering to read stories to her friends, trying to give them any comfort she could. She looked at all the bare walls and had an idea. She dusted off her old sewing machine, cleared the dining room table, bought some cloth and foam, and went back to work. Hanging Around was back as a non-profit business. Thanks to Ann, the walls in the clinic came alive.

On a chilly January morning in 1998, while at work, the place where I had shed so many tears before, the place that kept my mind occupied in positive ways, ever mindful of what was happening back home, I received a phone call.

"Hello, Mr. O'Shaughnessy, my name is Sheila. I run the children's oncology clinic at the hospital."

"Good morning Sheila. Ann has spoken often of you, very fondly I might add. I don't imagine you are calling with good news."

"Well, as you know, Ann was in today. She stopped by after her treatment and was reading books to the children. Mr. O'Shaughnessy, I am sorry to tell you this, but she had another seizure. While she was reading, she fell to the floor. She is in the emergency room right now."

I paused. I sighed. There was silence on the other end of the line. I took in a deep breath and exhaled the air that filled my lungs. I looked outside the window onto the highway and observed normalcy. People going about their business just like any other day.

"Thank you, Sheila, for calling me. That sounds just like Annie, as sick as she is, helping others. That's my girl, you know. Can you stay with her until I get there?"

"Yes, I'll be happy to."

"Thank you, I'll leave in a few minutes."

I finished what I needed to do and calmly left work. There was no sense in racing anymore. There was nothing to race to. Ann was in good hands and I knew what this meant. The lesions were back. They had never really left.

I broke no speed limits on the short drive to Ann Arbor, giving myself plenty of time to think, to absorb it all. To ponder how much time was left and to marvel at this woman I loved. What little time remained in her life, she was still giving. I reflected back on the rollercoaster ride that this had all been. The biopsy, the tears, the pain, the poison, and for the first time I began to question things that I was feeling inside of me.

I arrived and walked slowly, delaying the inevitable as long as I could. I announced who I was to someone who wanted to know and I was invited back to the cold sterile room with the same mild-colored linens I remembered from years ago. I'd been here before. I looked around and saw Ann, she saw me and smiled. My smile was weaker than hers; I leaned over, grabbed her hand, and kissed her forehead.

"Doctor says they're back. They must like me; they don't want to leave me alone."

"I know. What do they want to do?"

"They don't know yet, probably more radiation. And I was almost able to brush my hair again." She took her hand up against the side of her head, smiled again at me; it was a quick smile, one that she couldn't sustain. The dam broke in her eyes. I leaned in and hugged her, kissing her on the cheek. Words escaped me and a few tears of my own found their way out of my eyes, flowing down my cheeks as they had done so many times before.

I want you boys to be happy and content. To enjoy all the many wonderful things life offers. I hope that you both find a woman to love and have children. I know you'll both be successful.
A Mother's Journal
August 1995
Ann O'Shaughnessy

The volunteer and her little friends.
She made the straw doll.

21 | In the Winter She Talked About the Past

The past brought a smile back to Ann's face. Happier times reaching back on memories of her little ones scampering across the room, playing in the dirt or kicking a ball, it all brought back to her times when she was free again.

Soon, Ann was bald again. The fine grayish wisps that were beginning to sprout along the sides of her head were destroyed by the ghastly rays of poison. Seldom does anyone with Ann's condition ever receive two courses of full-brain radiation. It's not that they can't endure it, it's that they don't live long enough to see it.

Ann could now clearly see a line was forming. A line she was in. It was going somewhere, far enough away that she couldn't take anyone with her. In her final journey, Ann was going alone.

One of Ann's last projects was to leave her boys with a lasting image of her. Something they could hold onto long after she was gone. Long after she stopped being a mom, she thought she could still be a mother. She wanted me to help her with this last project, but my bravery fell short of this task. This gentle courageous woman, mired in a death march, was standing tall, while I cowered under the sheets. But like so many times before, Ann accepted my imperfections. Took them for what they were and nothing more than that, no judging, no animosity, just love.

For her last project, Ann made videotapes for her sons. These tapes spanned the course of several months during the last year of her life. Ann never stopped giving back. She pushed forward, slogging through the muck. It wasn't in her nature to sit around and hold pity parties for herself. She always thought no one would show up, so why bother? Plus, with whatever time God had left for her, she thought she may as well make the best of it.

It was February 12, 1998; the first videotaping had begun. Ann labeled the tape "A TAPE FOR ERIC IN THE FUTURE—XXXX-OOOO MOM." She sat in her favorite spot in the house, the place where our family gathered to watch television, open Christmas presents, or simply love on one another. The first taping she went alone, wearing a bandana to keep her head warm. Ever organized, she had note cards to keep her thoughts as clear as her mind would allow.

She had just come back from one more radiation treatment and on this day she talked about the past, things that she wanted Eric to know about himself, like when he was born small at six-and-a-half pounds with skinny little "chicken legs." When he was two months old she made him a baptismal dress, and she hoped that one day Eric's little boy or girl might wear the same dress.

> *Eric, you learned early, but you were not interested in learning your ABC's until you were about four and a half years old. We were going to Disney World and I said to you that you needed to learn your ABC's before we went and you did.*
>
> *There were so many things you and your brother did. Right from the beginning, you and your brother were best friends and that pleased your father and me so much. When you were about three, you had a little plastic rocking chair and you watched the Cinderella movie a hundred times. You loved that movie. You would always yell to me, "Mom, Mom, this is the part of her booti-ful dress." You couldn't say beautiful, you said bootiful. But this showed how artistic you were to notice the dress like that.*
>
> *When we lived in Texas, your grandmother would come to visit and as soon as she walked in the door you would grab her and*

take her to your play room. She could barely put down her luggage.
You'd push me away, close the doors, and for hours you and she
would play in this room. She is a great grandmother, and you and
she have always been close.

The tape stopped.

The past brought a smile back to Ann's face. Happier times reaching back on memories of her little ones scampering across the room, playing in the dirt or kicking a ball, it all brought back to her times when she was free again. Times when the things she thought about were the things she did, or would one day do; when she wasn't confined to living in the present and she could dream.

It was March 23, 1998, Eric's birthday. He was now twelve. It was also hat day. She dug into one of Eric's drawers and found an old jester's hat with penguins on it. She put it on her head and looked into the camera. "How do I look Eric? The store wanted twenty-five dollars, I made it for seven."

She was looking more and more like someone who was dying. She was beginning to slur her speech and her once razor-sharp memory was failing her.

But still she pushed on.

Before Eric was ten years old he had become an entrepreneur owning and operating a business in our basement. He called it "Bookbuster." He wrote books, mostly short stories, complete with drawings and autographs from the author. He charged his readers ten to fifteen cents and got all excited every time he sold a book to one of the neighbors. He started advertising about his business in monthly newsletters talking about what was coming up next. He sold them, too.

Bookbuster was non-profit, because the books were sold for far less than the paper cost. But what it did do was give a young child the chance to dream at a time when dreams were scarce and scary. It also gave a young mother the chance to see her son's imagination and artistry and the ability to look in the mirror knowing exactly where they came from.

On March 29, the taping continued. This day she had help. Collin was in his big chair, his blankie wrapped around him. Ann's baby was almost ten years old.

"Collin, does the blankie go on vacation with us?"

"Yes."

"What do you like to do with the blankie?"

"Smell it."

"Where do you smell it?"

He finds his favorite spot on the corner of the blanket.

"Right here."

It was probably a month or so ago in church when John's family was all here and Father George was giving the homily that day, which was very nice. And I am there, all of a sudden, messages started coming to me. A message of peace, of comfort, that John's family was next to us. John must feel good because his family hasn't come in, like, twelve years. And again I was just so peaceful and the strongest message I got was that God loved my children and He will watch over them, and then I got this overwhelming feeling that God just said to me, "Your husband loves you more than you know."

Ann's interview with Mary Mitsch
August 1998

She was more beautiful than the day we met.
She picked the wallpaper, it was green.

22 | LETTING GO

I could not remember the last time I had a belly laugh
without feeling guilty.

Despite cancer running unchecked through her body like a blaze on the scorched earth, life continued. There were soccer games to go to, band concerts, and dentist appointments. Friends were coming and going, rosary groups, healing masses, meetings with accountants and insurance people, and of course chemo and radiation treatments in a veiled attempt to keep Ann alive.

By March she began a new chemo: the last one she would ever take; Gemzar. It was the only one left. In April, she was fitted with a crown on her head. They dug holes in her skull in order to deliver precise and intense radiation to the tumors in her brain. It was all a shell game, because for every tumor they killed, two new ones were born. They were now in her spine. Ann was beginning to crumble like an old red barn. More radiation and even Ann thought perhaps, like

Sometimes all the best plans
and all the best intentions
never happen the way you
want them to.

her talent-show football player, she too could glow in the dark.

On May 14, Ann jotted a note in her calendar, "our fifteenth anniversary, doctor appointment 9:30." That same day after her visit, her doctor called me at work.

"Mr. O'Shaughnessy, how are you holding up?"

"One day at a time," I said.

"As you know, I saw Ann today. I don't like it when it comes to this point in the treatment process, but I believe at this time we need to stop all chemotherapy and radiation. She has taken all the agents for lung cancer and any more treatments would only further weaken her. What I'm concerned with now is her quality of life for her remaining days. You need to begin to look into a hospice program and we can help you with that. We made an appointment for next week and that is when I will tell your wife, but I wanted to give you some time to plan."

"Doctor, thank you for informing me. I knew this day would come sooner or later. But more importantly, thank you for all you have done for Ann."

"Well, she's a special lady. I have not seen anyone who fought as hard and long as she did. Can I count on you being with her next week?"

"Yes, I will."

Fifteen years ago we were returning from our honeymoon, two of the happiest people that walked the earth. I think Ann had the whole thing mapped out for us. We'd begin a family after a couple of years of just the two of us. We'd have two, maybe three children. We'd make enough money to own our own home, take a few vacations while watching our kids get bigger and bigger. We'd save for their college, eventually becoming grandparents when we were in our fifties. She'd dote over her grandchildren more than she did her own.

Sometimes all the best plans and all the best intentions never happen the way you want them to.

When the doctor gave me the news, I took it in stride. I didn't cry. The tears were gone. In some way I actually felt sorrier for him than me, the hardest part of his job had yet to come. He still had to tell Ann. I wondered, though, what had become of me. Where was my emotion? Where was my pain? What happened to my fight? It was then that I realized that I had hit a wall and I had become numb. It was then that I realized I was told to plan for a sprint but the sprint became a marathon. I was told to run as fast as I could, it wouldn't be far to go, but the target they were telling me to run to kept moving. They were all wrong and I was thankful they were wrong, but they were wrong and I was exhausted. It was then that I realized that everyone who came got to go home, rest, and recharge. Everyone except me.

We were now married fifteen years and one week. It was delightfully warm that day, much like the day this journey began almost three years ago. Another Michigan summer was almost upon us. The sun's rays trickled through the fresh tree buds and we traveled this same road that had brought us to this destination so many times before. I think I could have made this trip in my sleep.

But this time was different. This time I knew what was waiting for us. I think Ann was hopeful that the doctor had a different plan for her, a new unproven drug for her to try and I think she would have. I didn't have the heart to tell her why we were going. Maybe in the back of her brain, in between all the spots, she knew something wasn't right but if she did, she never let on.

Joyce and Arnie were back. I ask them to make another trip. They came whenever they were needed. They had arrived the day before, traveling through Canada, never the States. They'd stop at a casino or two along the way, trying to take their minds off things.

It had been a long road and Ann was slipping through our hands like buttered corn. The tides that once ebbed and flowed were now only ebbing, and every day the cancer consumed more and more of Ann, and what it took was irrevocable.

Her legs were dying. For long journeys, she had to resort to a wheelchair, bobbing around all hunched over. The Ann I knew detested losing control. But she was, and could do nothing about it. It was all part of this dreadful process: dying. We all knew she was slipping away. Ann knew it too, but she couldn't bring herself to believe it.

I don't remember one word that was spoken on this trip, perhaps none were.

The walk was made a little longer now as the oncology clinic had moved to a brand new building further away from the parking garage. Construction began shortly after we started coming here and I never thought we'd ever make the transition from old to new. But we did, Annie made it.

We walked along the long corridor just as we'd done so many times before, only now one of us wasn't walking. Three years I kept thinking, three years, it didn't seem it now. Where did they go? As soon as we got off the elevator, the nurses that had grown to love Ann now waited for her, and once they started crying and hugging Ann, my little secret was out.

We all squeezed into a conference room not much bigger than the bathrooms I lived in during the time here, but we made do. I pushed Ann in last, holding on to her shrinking hand, and waited for the doctor.

When I saw the door open, I braced myself.

"Hello, Mrs. O'Shaughnessy, how are you feeling today?"

From all the tumors and radiation, Ann's speech was fuzzy. "Not too good, I've had better days I guess."

"Well, it has been my sincere honor to have been your doctor."

Ann looked at him as if she knew the words that were about to come from his mouth, but yet it was still unimaginable that he was saying them to her.

"In my profession, unfortunately, I don't often get to know many patients like I have you. You have inspired so many people and I consider myself very lucky to have known you. You are a very special person to me and to everyone here who has come to know you.

"Medically speaking, Mrs. O'Shaughnessy, we have exhausted all treatment protocols. We have given you every chemo agent there is to fight this disease. I think any more treatments would only serve to weaken you further and would only shorten your life. I know these words are hard for you to hear and I am sorry to have to give them to you, however I believe it is in your best interest to stop all treatments and begin a hospice program."

Ann sat in her wheelchair, her shoulders arched forward letting his words sink in. Her eyes filled quickly with tears and sadness was draping her face.

"Will you still be my doctor?"

"I will."

"Are you saying I have less than six months to live?"

"I can never be sure about that, but I would say no more than six months. Our job now is to make whatever time that remains as comfortable for you as possible. I am sorry."

There was silence of words but not emotions. That, to me, meant the conversation was over. There was nothing left to say. He had more patients to see. I respected his time so I stood up and thanked the doctor for all he had done. He gave Ann one last embrace. Her hands were shaking, tears fell on her knees. He left Ann alone with her parents and me to ponder her future and what little remained of it.

As Ann's life neared its end, I was consumed by so many emotions. Anger and I parted ways a long time ago; it did me no good anymore. But sadness was stamped on my forehead, so was guilt. Sadness was palpable, someone I loved was about to leave me forever, I should be sad. But I didn't do well with the guilt. It had chased me like a rabid dog. It preyed on me like it would prey on a weak kitten. I could not remember the last time I had a belly laugh without feeling guilty. Any joy I felt over the last three years was tempered and short-lived.

I had given Ann all I had to give. From Day One I was in the fire with her, in the heat, up the hills and down the hills marching with her each step of the way. But now I was physically and emotionally exhausted. The tethered string once wrapped tightly around Ann's waist was losing its grip. Physically I was still with her and would never leave, but emotionally I was stepping aside. The present had bent this body of mine into a pretzel; in the future I thought I would unravel again.

23 | IN THE SUMMER SHE TALKED ABOUT HAPPINESS

Material things will not make you happy. Simple things will.

Months ticked off the calendar like dead leaves off a November tree. Hospice began coming to our house. They brought a hospital bed for Ann and it was placed on the first floor, in the dining room up against the inside wall. She fired the first three nurses who didn't show up on time. "Don't they know my time is valuable?" Her balance became shaky, walking on legs half the size they were before the badness began. Her world, once liberated, was now restricted to wherever someone would take her.

By June, I think Ann knew the last room her life would ever know was the dining room.

Knowing Ann, the whole reason behind the videotapes was to talk to the boys as only a mother can, about the future, a future she knew she would never see. In the July tape with Eric's name on it, she talked about sex and she talked about love. She told him to stay focused on school and she laughed when she told him to "wait until you're at least twenty-five before you get married."

For the Fourth of July we had visitors from Massachusetts. My sister and her daughters came. They came three years too late. I was disappointed with my sister and so was Ann. "Why doesn't your sister come to visit us, John? I would love to see her girls. Doesn't she know I'm dying?"

She knew Ann was dying and I'm not sure why she waited so long. We made the best of it though and we were gracious enough, but by now, my patience for some people was running thin. I was labeling people. I wasn't proud of this. But people who failed to get in the game with us, or at least walk the sidelines every now and then, I labeled "scorekeepers." My sister was a scorekeeper, calling in every now and then, learning the score of Ann's condition, throwing back pleasantries that I failed to catch. A scorekeeper just couldn't suit up three years later and expect all would be well. She wasn't alone, there were others, but thank goodness all these years later, not a moment went by when either Ann or I ever felt alone.

By July her wheelchair had become her main form of getting around. Collin took it upon himself to entertain his mother at a time when she needed it most, and so when Ann wasn't using the wheelchair, Collin was, pirouetting around the house in his new four-wheeled toy. He also decided he needed a pet. Two pet newts joined the O'Shaughnessy family. Tom and Jerry were their names.

By the end of July, Ann began to look into the camera and talk in past tense more and more. A few gray hairs had begun to sprout along the sides of her head, not enough to make much of a difference, but who cared anyway?

> *Eric, all I ask is that you push yourself to do well. You have been blessed by God. Remember that material things will not make you happy. Simple things will. I am proud of you and I love you.*

There was nothing Ann loved more than her flesh and blood, those boys, our boys. I knew that and I accepted that and I loved that about her. But still, she made me feel loved too. It was her unique gift to make the person she was with at that very moment feel loved by the words she spoke.

It was August 20, 1998. Ann wore her wig on this day so Collin would know what she looked like with hair. Again she sat alone in the living room pushing the button to start the camera and walked ever so slowly into the camera's view. This was Collin's tape—she labeled it "COLLIN, I AM WATCHING YOU. I LOVE YOU, MOM."

> *Collin, I always loved children. Wherever we have lived I would organize events that involved getting kids together. I loved doing that. I always thought I would be a great grandmother. People wanted me to work, but I thought my job was my boys and I am glad I did that. You are such good kids and we have had a great family. Collin, you adore Eric and that pleases me very much. Remember Collin, money can't buy happiness. Look at me, I could win the lottery tomorrow and what would I have? God doesn't care how much money you have.*

She paused after that last statement and began to sob. Before stopping the tape she told Collin she loved him.

In September, Ann completed what she started and did it in a way that was all Ann: simple, eloquent, to the point, and without the drama that was filling her dwindling days on earth. The tape was much like Ann's life now, blurry, fuzzy, fading in and out, but still filled with love. She was upstairs in Eric's bedroom, holding this camera that now weighed almost what she did. She spread his football jersey on the bed, turned the camera on and began to film nothing else but a green jersey, talking as the camera rolled, unfocused, thinking, I'm sure, and wondering to herself, "*Will I ever see him wear this?*"

Lastly, she read a poem.

> *One of the people I love the most*
> *Never pushes or shoves*
> *She is always willing and bright*
> *And never causes a fight*
> *One of the people I care for most, a person for whom I care*
> *Doesn't even have any hair*
> *But looks do not matter, she is beautiful anyway*

She may be the prettiest mother of her day
One of the people I love to hug and kiss
Would never sit around and miss
She tries new things and sees the world
Through the eyes of a girl
Merry Christmas,
Mom

"Eric, this is what I am talking about. These are the gifts that make people happy."

The tape ended. Her last project was complete.

I feel overwhelmed at times when I really think about how blessed I am. All the people that God has placed in our lives, the support, you know I feel like, why me? It's overwhelming. I have five hundred cards from people in Plymouth and I have kept every one.
   Ann's interview with Mary Mitsch
   Summer 1998

This is the rosary group that was formed to pray for Ann: Mary Beth, Claudia, Mary Ann, Kathy, Mary Ann, Sue, Irene, Ann, Sharon, and Father Jim.

24 | On Good Days She Saw Grown Men

I think God let her peek into the future and see her boys as grown men. She saw them laughing freely just like they were now, only they were more joyful, like something had been lifted from their boots.

Long before Ann's legs began to fail her and she could walk freely, she passed by our refrigerator and stopped in her tracks. A simple white piece of paper with phone numbers of friends and family was held to the ice box with a couple of free magnets, the kind from the pizza shops and insurance companies. They were there in case the boys needed someone to call when I wasn't around. Most were typed, a few late additions were handwritten in the color of ink most readily available. One name and number stood out and got Ann's attention. The name and number of this friend was scrolled in orange ink. The name was GOD and the phone number was P-R-A-Y-E-R.

Eric wrote it.

On August 9, a steamy Sunday, we had traveled four hours to retrieve our sons, who had spent the last two weeks at summer camp in northern Michigan. We had missed them. Ann had an unsteady gait. She walked as if stones were in her shoes. I held her arms to help balance her but I feared if she fell, her arm might go with her. The wheelchair was of no use at camp, the paths were all bumpy, littered with rocks and roots. She was weak and would soon be forty-two years old, but looked far older. Still she smiled. Her green bandana matched her green shorts. No one, including Ann, thought she would make it to camp. The slippery slope in recent weeks had become steeper and she was sliding further and quicker into a deep dark hole. But somehow, for a few days anyway, she climbed her way out of this hole. It was as if she knew something special was waiting for her.

And if she didn't know, someone else did.

"Are you Mr. and Mrs. O'Shaughnessy?"

"Yes, we are."

"'I've heard so much about you from your son. I am Eric's counselor, also Erik, but with a 'k'. It's a pleasure to meet you. I just want to say you have a special young man there. I could tell from the time I met him that he is a leader. You can tell that you both have made him your highest priority. He is a great kid."

"Thank you, Erik. I love your name." Ann's speech was more rasping and garbled. "You've told me something I already knew but it's always good to hear those words again. Thank you."

The boys kept in touch with us, little dollops of sunshine they were, writing home, telling us about their various wilderness adventures. When not in the woods or in their cabins, they ventured off to Mackinac Island and went shopping with money we had given them. They sat around camp fires and sang new songs they learned. Eric, ever the big brother, kept a careful watch over Collin. It was Eric who talked Collin into going at all. But I wondered the whole time they were there if they were thinking about their dying mother back home. I hoped they were smiling, laughing even, mixing it up with new friends washing clean all that was stripping them of their precious childhood and what remained of it.

July 31, 1998

Hey,

Did you give me 3 postcards? That's all I see. Anyway, we're having a good time at camp. The rest of the guys in my cabin seem to be too. I found Skip. He has long hair this year. I think we traded haircuts. Erik and John (my counselors) are really fun guys. Collin seems to be having fun too. The front of this card is probably dirty it's because I am writing on the wood. They fixed the bed, no more wobbly.

That's all,

Love, Eric

Dear Mom and Dad,

You have been writing a lot. All is going well. Tell Zach I am in St. Charles with Eric Swanson and John C. from Columbia. There is a lot of new stuff here. Jim said we would do Snitsehauk tonight. Erik is a wonderful storyteller. I am still a beginner rider. After rest I have boat and/or fish then ride. I have a great cabin, that has made the trip better this year than last. If Collin hasn't already told you we have two O'Shaughnessy honor campers this year. Now I have to be off to the lake.

Love, Eric

Dear Mom and Dad,

On the first letter things were real bad. It was only the third day. Things are really a lot better now. I made a lanyard and I love horseback riding. My cabin has been winning the junior cabin cleanup. And you want to see something cool, I won first week honor camper. I plan on coming back next year. Amen.

Love, Collin

P.S. See you in a week.

Later that evening at church, the last night of camp, Ann got to see her boys sing. Collin learned a new song, "Here I Am, Lord." There were hundreds of young boys at this camp in all age groups from about seven to seventeen. They went to church twice a day, they ate well, they fished and frolicked among the birds and the grass. Late at night they told stories in their cabins before they drifted off to sleep.

But after Mass was why Ann came. It was awards time. Prizes were given for camper of the year and runner-up. They were based on teamwork, hustle, participation, leadership, and attitude. After the seven- and eight-year-old awards were given, Collin's counselor was called up. We knew at least that someone in Collin's cabin had won an award. I looked at Ann and I was looking at someone who was just happy to be there at all. She was with her boys in the presence of God.

Collin's counselor spoke. "The first award I want to give is for honor camper of the year runner-up in the junior age group. For this young man, it was his first camp and though he was a little shy at first, he came around in the second week and really excelled. It was my pleasure to be his counselor this summer. Runner-up award goes to Collin O'Shaughnessy."

Our baby beamed with pride and strutted to the altar to receive his trophy. We were beaming with pride, too. Ann watched his every move and a tear fell down her cheek. She smiled and it dripped on her white blouse. Everyone in church was clapping for our son, and some who had figured out his mother was Ann and she was dying, clapped all the harder.

A few minutes passed, other awards were given and then it was time for the intermediate age group and Eric's counselor approached the altar.

"It is my pleasure to announce the honor camper of the year. I could tell the moment I met this young man that he was a special kid and a leader. He did everything that was asked of him, he helped his teammates, and he did it all with a great attitude. Honor camper of the year, 1998— Eric O'Shaughnessy."

More and more people had it figured out now. They could tell from the look Ann gave when the name O'Shaughnessy was called. People were clapping very loudly. Ann and I were not the only ones whose eyes flowed with tears.

When it was all over, we embraced our young men. We laughed and we cried some more, and told them how proud we were of them. Then we retraced the four hours back home, never to return to camp again. The boys sat in the back seat of the car, laughing a few times and talking extensively about their busy fourteen days. The horseback rides, the soccer games, the bonfires, and how wonderful it all was. Their energy seemed boundless, they were "wound like a top," as my mother used to say about me. Poor Ann could have used some of that energy. Not long after the car door closed, she was sleeping. I glanced over at her, this lady I loved, her silhouette slouched under the black sky and the twinkling stars. I let my mind wander to happier times, times when my driftwood was circling trying to find some warm dry land. Times when all that we quarreled over was what movie to rent and all that disappointed us was another Boston Red Sox baseball season. My mind wouldn't let me stray far though, it was like it was umbilically attached to the moment I was in. Driving south on the highway, headlights glued to the road, weary as I was, it quickly pulled me back to the womb of my life, a womb that even I sometimes wanted to escape from.

Still, somehow, fighting with myself and the road, it occurred to me that this short trip amid the rocks and the roots, the stars and the trees, had given Ann all she needed. Once again, I think God stepped in and peeled away the clouds and let her peek into the future to see her boys as grown men. She saw them laughing freely just like they were now, only they were more joyful, like something had been lifted from their boots. I think she saw them going to dances with pretty girls on their arms, becoming captains of football teams, graduating from schools, and seeing parts of this big world she never would.

I think Ann maybe knew all along why she got to go on this trip and at that moment, her little secret, if that's what it was, was safe with me. Fading forward, maybe not so warm, or dry, but safe.

All of a sudden, Eric started talking. He said, "Well, I'm telling you, Mom, about a dream I had. It was pretty amazing." I said, "What are you talking about?" And then he started talking about his dream and he was drowning. He said, "I was under and I couldn't get up and then there was this bright light. I think it was orange and I knew I wasn't going to make it." And I said, "Eric, how scary." He said, "No, Mom, it wasn't scary at all."

Ann's interview with Mary Mitsch
Summer 1998

25 | GOOD FRIENDS

Some people run away from the fire, others run to it, some just admire the flames and do nothing at all.

As autumn approached, the wind was leaking more from my sails. Like Ann, I was losing speed in my steps. It felt like she was on my shoulders and these hills I'd climbed with her had grown steeper. Just like at camp, rocks littered my path or what path there was. It felt more like an uncharted path and my walk felt more like a lumber. If Ann was descending into a deep dark hole, then I was descending with her, only I didn't want to go.

The fall calendar was busy. Life continued, time marched on, it didn't even slow down. Eric began playing football but broke his arm in the fourth game. Ann got upset with me when I was impatient waiting four hours to have his arm set. Collin had weekend soccer games. Ann had rosary groups to attend. New furniture was being delivered that Ann would hardly get to use. Mass services were being conducted in friend's homes. Pam came from hospice once a week to care for Ann and monitor her steady decline. Ann finally allowed me to get a cleaning lady; she, too, came every week. The boys saw a therapist and they talked about, what else, death.

Friends from all over came every day. Kathy Boyer (Cross), her old roommate from years ago, traveled several hundred miles on Halloween night to care for Ann. It wasn't like old times though, she was working on her and taking caring of her in a way she never thought she would. Debbie and Mary Lou from Texas did the same thing. It was all a magical orchestration of schedules, as one arrived, one gave a sad farewell and Ann was still behind it all.

On October 15, we celebrated Ann's forty-second birthday as best we could. It was a chilly day and the leaves had begun their descent to earth, matting down the grass. Joyce and Arnie had returned from a couple of weeks away and the time they got to recharge was getting shorter. We sang "Happy Birthday," we lit candles and ate cake. Ann sat at the table in her wheelchair, her eyes increasingly more glazed, her shrinking body increasingly more thin, but still she smiled. She let Collin blow the candles out.

The dining room was arranged the way Ann wanted it. Her bed was against the inside wall close to the kitchen so she could eavesdrop on some casual conversation going on in there. Her wheelchair was close by her bed. The oak dining table where she once made her wall hangings was pushed to the other side of the room. Pictures of Eric and Collin adorned a shelf. Morphine on demand was now keeping her comfortable. An oxygen tank connected to her nose and helped her breathe. More tubes connected to her, some carried fluids out, and others sent them in. She clung to a rosary that someone gave her. There were books and cards from well-wishers scattered about the room waiting for someone to organize them.

By early November, the days were getting shorter. Darkness now draped over us when we were eating dinner. Cool crisp air was now replaced by a cold dampness. Pam informed me that Ann had turned a corner. Her body was shutting down. It wouldn't be long now, a week or two but no more than that. She asked if I had all her affairs in order and said that if there were any last-minute plans I needed to make, I should make them soon.

With the corner now turned, one last person needed to visit Ann; her best friend from Boston, Laureen Goguen. With Laureen and her husband Brian, Ann and I had been on many vacations together, usually someplace warm where Ann could bask and bake, while I just burned. The same sun, just different results. I'd go home with blisters and cream all over me, Annie would be a goddess. But, oh, the laughs we all enjoyed. A few cocktails and we'd turn back the clock and acted like the fools we were.

The night Laureen arrived, it was as black as the underside of the sea.

"So how's my buddy doing, John?" asked Laureen. "Will she know who I am?"

"I'm not sure, Laureen. I guess she will, but it all depends on how she is feeling at that moment. She no longer sees real well, but maybe she will remember your voice. All I know is it's great to have you here with us. Ann always wanted you to be with her near the end."

"And I promised her I would. It's hard to believe three and a half years have passed."

"I know, but the last few months have been real tough for all of us. I think we are all ready to say our goodbyes."

"Have the boys said goodbye yet?"

"No, they haven't."

We drove home and talked the whole way. How blessed I felt to have an old friend to help her best friend, my wife. We arrived home and were greeted by Joyce and Arnie, who hadn't left their daughter for a few weeks now. They embraced Laureen, but Laureen quickly began to search for her friend and found her sitting quietly in her wheelchair in the dining room.

"How ya doing?" Ann mumbled to Laureen.

"I'm doing great, how are you doing?"

"I've been better."

"Well, I told you I'd be here, didn't I?"

"Yeah, but I was worried I wouldn't be."

"Well, I knew you would be. You can't go anywhere yet; we have some catching up to do."

"You want to catch up and I want to go back. I wish I could you know. We had some happy times didn't we, Laureen?"

"Yes we did, Annie, we sure did. I'll always have them, you know. The memories—I get to keep them. They're tucked away somewhere safe, close to my heart. You'll always be right here."

"No, I won't, I'll be up there!"

As Laureen removed her hand from her heart, Ann limply pointed her index finger toward the ceiling and the sky and heaven. Both, I thought, were saying the same thing. All three of us sat and talked, catching up on recent events and old times. Even though it made more sense to cry, we forced out a laugh or two.

Ann helped us do that.

Eric is quiet, but he is very connected to God. Once he was asking me questions about a support group and stuff, and I said, "Eric, are you concerned if something happened today, what would you do?" And we talked about that and he said, "Mom, we just have to trust that God wouldn't let lighting strike twice." He said, "The hardest thing will be the first time we're out, the three of us, when we go to cross the street and we see a family with a mother. I think that will be really hard." But he continued with, "You know, Mom, we have to be grateful for the time we had with you. God has given us so much."

Ann's interview with Mary Mitsch
Summer 1998

26 | Goodbyes Bring Peace

"Mom, it's okay for you to go be with God. We will miss you, but we'll be okay. I am glad I had twelve years with you and you were a great mom for Collin and me. You don't have to hang on anymore. You can let go."

Ann wanted to be cremated. It was something she had discussed with me on a couple of occasions. She was firm on that. She cleared it first with Father George, though. She wanted to make sure God didn't have a problem with it. He didn't. She did not want to be stuck in some pine box six feet below. She thought it was "too cold down there."

She had plenty of time to plan her funeral, too. She wanted everything at the church. The funeral home had one job, to make her pretty. Close friends could stop by early, but the casket was to be open for no more than one hour, then I was to close it. She chose the songs, who would sing them, and the order they would be sung. "Here I Am, Lord" was to be the opening hymn, "Gentle Woman" would be sung during the presentation of gifts, and "Ave Maria" during communion. The last song was "On Eagles' Wings" and she gave everyone

Her body was now a mere vessel that she would soon shed and leave behind. Like a butterfly, she would fly away.

permission to cry then and she predicted we would. She said she would be watching and would take names of anyone who didn't.

Ann would never walk again. She now needed help to get from her wheelchair into bed. Her world was getting smaller, closing in on her like thick plaque on hard arteries. The tumors in her head had almost blinded her and the ones in her spine almost paralyzed her. Her body was now a mere vessel that she would soon shed and leave behind. Like a butterfly, she would fly away.

Outside in the cool air, the boys played in the front yard wearing sweat-shirts and blue jeans to keep them warm. Ann was in her wheelchair in the dining room catching up on old times and sipping tea with her best friend. Arnie and Joyce were watching television in the family room.

This was the day, I thought, for goodbyes. I brought the boys inside, sat them down in the library, and closed the door behind them.

"Guys, I need to talk with you about your mom. Have you noticed that she is getting weaker every day now?"

Collin waited for Eric's lead. They both nodded in agreement.

"Your mom doesn't want to leave you guys. She fought so hard for so long. We need to give her our permission to go be with God. Do you think you can do that?"

Again they nodded. We hugged together for a few minutes. I was bursting with sadness, for them, for me, and most of all for Ann.

"I want you both to know that I love you very much and I will do everything I can to help you through this. Continue to pray to God and ask for His help as well."

They looked at me with their small faces. Eric fully comprehended what I said and knew what he needed to do. I think Collin thought he would just follow his brother's lead and do whatever he did: listen, nod, and maybe even cry.

"Your mom will be sad and may cry. It's okay for you to cry too. This is a very sad time and it's not fair that you two boys are losing your mom. You have done so well for so long and I love you both and your mom loves you so much." Tears broke free from my eyes and now dribbled down my face.

"We're ready if you are, Dad."

"Eric, you're a brave young man. Collin, are you okay?"

"I'm okay, Dad."

The walk wasn't far, through the front foyer and the living room, and as we looked to our right, there was Ann. She was in her bed pushed up against the wall. The oxygen tank was on and tubes ran up her nose, but she beamed as she always did whenever she saw the boys. She hadn't been out of bed in days and her vision was cloudy but she could see their outlines and knew it was them coming to see her. Her "little men," as Ann use to call them.

"Hi, Mom," said Eric. They both gave her a gentle, loving embrace, trying not to inflict any more pain on her. She cupped her hand on each face, smiling, bringing them in closer to her, looking at them through her clouds, wanting to rewind her clock. They both latched on to one of her hands sitting as close to her as they could.

The words I needed to tell her were words she didn't want to hear. These next few minutes I knew would be excruciating for her, and for me and our sons, but nothing about anything these days was easy.

"Annie, the boys and I have been talking and I know you will not like to hear this, but I feel they need to say goodbye to you. Can you understand this?" From the foot of the bed I gave Eric an approving nod, telling him to proceed.

"Mom, I love you."

"I love you too, Mom," replied Collin in a softer tone.

"It's okay for you to go be with God. We will miss you, but we'll be okay. I am glad I had twelve years with you and you were a great mom for Collin and me. You don't have to hang on anymore. You can let go."

Her mouth began to quiver and then it broke and as she tried to push out some words. Words that I'm sure she thought about often over the course of time. Long flowing tears covered her face and it began to turn red. Her speech was broken and suspended by pauses when she wiped her nose or eyes. "Boys I love you too, more than you'll ever know . . . I want you to promise me to do well with your life. Be nice to people and they will be nice to you . . . I wish I could have seen you grow old; I tried my best . . . But I'll always watch over you when I'm in heaven."

The boys leaned over their mom and hugged her, not wanting to let go.

She wrapped her weakened arms around them. I leaned over all three of them and my emotions swelled.

"I never liked goodbyes." Her face was now covered with tears. "But this one is so lasting. I will see you again one day in heaven and I hope for you it's a long time from now. I hope you grow up and have children of your own some day. You'll both be good fathers. And you know, boys, Dad is still here for you and he will help you through this."

Our sons were glued to every word Ann spoke. Their innocence had long since been taken away by this disease that was taking their mother's life, but now it was gone; peeled back like bark from a dying tree, never to return again.

"We know, Mom. We love you." Eric reached in again for her hand and then let go. Her little men walked away.

I stayed.

"Ann, I love you too. Always have and always will. You have been a great mother and a loving wife. You have always been there. I want you to know that you will be missed by everyone. I will be the best dad I can be to our sons. I will do what I can to make sure we are all fine. My career will not come before them. I promise you I won't let you down."

"You'll find someone when I'm gone, won't you?" she asked rhetorically.

"Ann, I intend to be happy again one day and I hope that I am lucky enough to find someone as good as you were. It won't be easy, you know."

"I know," she replied with a smug look. "Stay close to God and He will help you and the boys like He has helped me all these years."

Because of your help, the boys and I have learned to live our lives, know that you will always be with us in spirit.

"I will. You know I love our sons with all my heart."

"I know that. I have never doubted that," she replied. "And I also know I am being replaced by a dog."

"How did you know that?"

"Collin told me."

"Well, he has asked for one for a long time so I suppose one day I may need to break down and get him one. In due time, it will all work out. It's all right for you to go. Tell God you are ready to come see Him and live with Him. Because of your help, the boys and I have learned to live our lives. Know that you will always be with us in spirit." I paused. I gave Ann time to try to absorb all that had been handed to her.

"Ann, I have written your eulogy, and if you like I will read it to you."

She nodded her head approvingly and I moved a little closer to her. I invited Laureen and Joyce to come join us. I composed myself, looked into her eyes, and began to read.

In Her Life

I never dreamed I would be here before you today. I never dreamed my children would lose their mother. I never dreamed I would lose my wife. All of you never dreamed you would lose such a dear friend, a sister, and a daughter.

But let us rejoice for having known her if only for a short time or her entire life. Let us remember how she blessed us all. Her children learned from her how to love, how to be kind and considerate to each other. We learned from her the gift of time unto others without time unto ourselves. We learned about thoughtfulness and compassion. We learned about spirituality.

In her life she made us laugh. She made us believe in ourselves when others did not. In her life she had the patience of a saint. She showed us how to be strong. In her life she always tried to be right and seldom was she wrong.

In her life she bore a son, Eric. He will carry on her passion to love, to give your best and to pursue your dreams. In her life she bore another son, Collin, who will carry on and live her legacy for kindness, for humor and spirit. Their life with their mother, though far too short, was long enough to last forever.

Now we must all turn the page and live what she has taught us. To think fondly of times before the hurt, of life before the sadness. There were many, many good times in her life. Treasure your memories deep in your heart. For in the end we must all seek another day, so each of us may find our way.

God bless you.

She looked up at me, nodded her head ever so slightly, and smiled. "That's good," she said.

At this point in Ann's brain, I think the bad cells outnumbered the good, but despite that she was fighting through and I think she was seeing her funeral unfold.

Thousands of people would read her obituary and hundreds would mark their calendars. Word would spread, *Ann O'Shaughnessy, 42, beloved wife of John, loving mother of Eric and Collin.* It would be a mild fall evening, the wind would be calm, and men would wear suit coats, women, light jackets. Her mom would cry, as would her dad, but so wouldn't everyone? Her boys would look handsome in sharp attire purchased just for this occasion, a nice tie, maybe a sweater and black pants. She knows they will never wear them again. They will be nervous but brave as they enter the church, I will hold their hands. They will walk cautiously up to the casket where she lay. They will look inside and see her. Close friends and family would arrive. Some would reach in and touch her cold body. All would say a prayer. She would look pretty, but the picture of her taken months before would sit close by to remind everyone of the Ann they once knew. After a while of milling around and reminiscing, Eric and I would be instructed to close the casket, her family would take one last look, Collin would be fearful, but comforted by someone who loved him.

Songs would be sung just as she planned them. Readings would be read. Three priests would preside over her funeral. Then I would eulogize her and everyone would be wiping away tears.

Over the next few days, life finally did slow down. Fewer friends came by. For most, it was too painful to see the withered shell of the woman they had grown to know and love. They wanted to remember her differently. So they stayed away and waited for a phone call.

Dear John,
February 4, 1997

I am so saddened. The tears flow down my face. What a mess, I think, and how did I get this way?

I have been writing the letters to the children. How can I convey such deep love for them? My goals in life have been filled. To be a wife, have a home and children. Yet I am not ready for it to be over. Little Collin is only eight, it breaks my heart. A little sweet kid like that needs a mom, how can I be taken away from him?

Your role as a parent has been doubled. You still can be impatient and hot tempered. You need to seek out and obtain my traits, patience and understanding. The boys need to know that you are approachable, that they can come to you with anything. You need to forgo your needs and focus on theirs. They are my blood too and it's your final gift to me to care for them in every way. I know how very much you love them, I have no doubt about that.

I worry about your impatience and when you are tired. It's a huge role to be both parents. It will be your cross to carry. Ask for God's constant help and guidance. I have carried this diagnosis around for eighteen months now and it never leaves my mind. It's harder than anyone can know. It's not the drugs, or the illness, it's the fact that the end is near. Maybe one to five years, it's still too short. I try so hard to seek joy in every day and I look to God for help.

I am sure my death will be overwhelming for you. The cross will be passed from me to you. How angry I feel and how awful to know the pain I gave you. Our pain is great because of the love we had.

Never when I took those vows, "till death do we part," did I think it would mean only fourteen years. Please know John that you fulfilled my every dream. I was never a modern woman. I loved being home and you offered me that. We had a rich family life and I am glad we had many vacations together.

John, I love you.

27 | THE VIGIL: HOLDING ON

Some things are entombed secrets.

"I'm trying to die, you know. My best friend has to go back to work."

Every morning in those final fleeting days, after a night of restlessness, I came downstairs and feared going into the dining room. I'd often wait for Laureen or Joyce to get up first and then wait to hear voices, soft sounds of women speaking to one another. Conversations which I couldn't understand, but if I didn't get a knock on my door, I knew this wasn't the day.

It was cowardly of me, I know. Part of me had said goodbye and let her go while part of me was holding on to her every last breath. This part of me didn't want to let her go. It wanted the tide to go out and come back in again, just like it had done so many times before.

But go she must. Even Ann understood that. The door was opening for her. Her friend needed to go back to work and back to her husband who was waiting ever so patiently back in Boston for a phone call. Her parents needed to go home to Darien. I needed to attempt to be a single dad. Her sons needed to find their way in a motherless world.

There was no choosing any of this. It was all happening; there was no stopping it. Time for Ann was running out. Our time with her was slipping away. Her stop was coming soon.

"I can't even die right," she'd say to us. "I guess God doesn't want me yet. He must have other people more ready than me. But look at me! Who can be more ready than I am? I can't see, I can't move. I need help breathing, and this morphine drip says it all. Don't I look like I'm ready?"

She did look ready, every day a little more. She kept her sense of humor with us though, right to the bitter end, right to her last puff of air. Her mind was ready, but her body wasn't. Not yet, anyway. It was wiggling its way into place getting ready for the last step off the cliff.

One morning, I just knew something was different. I came downstairs and didn't hear women talking. Instead of turning right into the dining room, I turned left into the kitchen where Joyce and Arnie were sitting at the table. Joyce was sipping some coffee. Arnie didn't look up, but Joyce did and her gaze said everything.

"She didn't wake up this morning, John. Maybe she'll wake up later. She's still breathing, but her eyes won't open. I guess she's sleeping in today."

Through the kitchen I walked into the dining room to see Ann. Her face was ashen gray, her mouth wide open inhaling and exhaling, making struggled sounds. She looked like she was sleeping; perhaps, maybe having a bad dream. Her heart, one of the few organs that remained working, kept circulating blood through her almost lifeless body.

There she was, the shell of this beautiful woman I loved, a butterfly waiting to escape. And here I was again, driftwood, circling, spinning, taking on too much water, the currents over the last three years long since having gotten the best of me. I couldn't take much more of seeing my girl this way, weak and blurry eyed, fighting for every breath. A weary lost soul I was, on a lazy stream, Annie by my side and a black labyrinth ahead. She was waiting perhaps for the right moment when she could look at me one last time, blow me a kiss, and slip away. She rescued me once, a long time ago, but I remembered it like it was last week. I would have loved to have rescued her from this thing, but controlling this was about as difficult as pushing the sun. Some things are entombed secrets.

And so the currents and I battled one last time. Off in the distance was the thunderous roar of a waterfall, but beyond that was silence. Peace for Ann, a tranquil space. I would let her go, and after that, grab an old tree limb and swim to shore where two young boys were waving their arms, begging me to find them.

28 | SHE WAS EVERYWHERE

She was everywhere, but nowhere. Not sitting next to me, anyway.
That's where I wanted her: healthy, vibrant, her hair pulled
back wearing something pretty, reaching for my hand telling me
everything would be all right.

On November 17, an unusually warm fall afternoon, at slightly after one o'clock when the dining room for the first time in weeks was vacant, Ann took her last breath and died. It had been days since she last moved. Thank God we all had said goodbye before her last flight came, the flight that took her home.

Her friends, Laureen and Mary, were close by, as were Joyce and Arnie. The boys were at school. I was pretending to work when Laureen called me and told me to come home. I think it was all just as she wanted it to be. I think she wanted to go alone, peacefully with no one around, including me.

I raced home as if I could somehow catch her last breath. It reminded me of 1995, when I raced home to get the bad news, the genesis of it all, forty-one months ago.

I came home and found Ann wearing her wig. Her cold hands were folded over her chest. Her lips were blue. I wondered if her spirit was floating above us or was already gone. Joyce, Laureen, and I all stood over her and stared at her lifeless body. I don't know why.

The hospice nurse pronounced her dead and the funeral home was called. The funeral director came, the one Ann had met with to go over all the plans. "Make me pretty," she had said to him. He came with help and a big black bag that zippered in the front. Ann was going in that bag. Soon they would have my wife back at their laboratory doing things to her that I didn't want to think about.

I gathered the boys from school. As soon as they heard the call to come to the front office they knew why. It was now the three of us driving home, quiet and somber, aching all over. When we got home they wanted to give their mom one last thing to take with her. Eric found a coffee cup that he had bought her that said, "The world's best MOM." Collin found a picture of him and her. They both were smiling then.

Brave boys they were.

I made phone calls to friends and family, telling them about Ann and how she died in her sleep, peacefully. She had put up such a good fight, I had said to them. You know she loved you very much and she is no longer in any pain. Her suffering is over, she is gone now. We must all move on without her. As hard as that will be, she would want that for all of us.

The next couple of days I never stopped thinking about Ann, her body back at the morgue. I had to visit there a couple of times to pick out the casket, drop off the clothes she would wear, and sign some forms. Her body was just a few feet away from me, locked away in some room. I hoped they were taking good care of her.

I couldn't yet fathom that the day had come and I was a widower. It was all so surreal.

The boys and I went to J.C. Penney to buy clothes. I had never bought them clothes before, Ann had always done that. I picked out a few outfits and I could hear her telling me, *No, not that one, John, try another one, it doesn't fit Collin, it's too big on him.* I kept parading in and out of racks looking for sizes and colors that I thought she would approve of. Not too bright and cheery, but not too morbid either. Here I was still trying to please her, her dead body being made pretty, the burden of everything now placed heavy on my shoulders, but Ann was lifting that burden for the time being, talking me through this new task. I finally found something she seemed to like, or at least she told me she did. *They look handsome, John, you did well.*

I wondered if she'd always talk to me this way. Would I always hear her gentle whispers telling me what to do? Reminding me of things I was likely to forget, like measles shots and school assignments, or would her voice fade away like a cloud pushed by the wind only seen once, and never again? I hoped to hear her voice often, I still needed her help.

The funeral was two nights later at St. John Neumann's church in Canton. It was a pleasant fall evening; the sun was just setting, casting an orange glow over the church. The entire service was there, the wake, the funeral, everything, a three-hour celebration of her life, not her death.

Family and close friends came early. The church was dark. I walked in holding the boys' hands, one on each. They looked handsome in sweater vests, black pants, white shirts, and ties. A bright light was shining down on the casket that contained their mother. We all walked slowly to this space and as we got closer I could feel Collin's grip on my hand get tighter, his little palms more moist. We looked inside this box. I touched her hand one last time and kissed her forehead. Eric did too. The portrait taken eighteen months ago for this one occasion was framed and displayed on a table nearby. It wasn't needed, she looked pretty.

My family came. I was disappointed that not all of them came. A brother-in-law and sister-in-law were missing, but I was grateful for who was there. We all stayed near Ann, filling ourselves with last glimpses of her.

The boys stayed close to me and me to them. Little Collin Patrick wouldn't let me go. His mother was in a box and he couldn't bear to look at her anymore. He had said his goodbyes and now he just wanted to go home, crawl into bed, and cry for about a week or two. But people kept pouring in and he couldn't go home, not yet.

Father George was there; in fact three priests presided over Ann's service, just as she thought they would. Somehow they all worked it out amongst themselves. They all loved her.

Again Ann spoke to me. *John, it's been an hour, it's time to say goodbye again. Close the lid.* My oh my, what a great wife she was, still now keeping me in line, keeping me on task.

People were piling in by the hundreds, but Ann wanted them to see the live portrait of her, not the dead image of her. Not the shell that was now her, pretty as she was. So Eric and I closed the door and said farewell.

People started singing, *I, the Lord of sea and sky, I have heard my people cry. All who dwell in dark and sin, my hand will save. I, who made the stars of night, I will make their darkness bright. Who will bear my light to them? Whom shall I send? Here I am, Lord. Is it I Lord? I have heard you calling in the night. I will go Lord, if you lead me, I will hold your people in my heart.*

The more people sang, the more they cried, just as Ann wanted it to be.

I eulogized her again, but this time she didn't hear me the same way she did before. At the pulpit, I looked out over the throngs of people who had gathered. Not a dry eye to be found. Ann's closed casket to my left, our boys a few feet in front of me, and I spoke, looking up after every few words.

I don't know where I found the strength but I pushed through. Maybe Ann was with me still.

I never dreamed I would be here before you today. I never dreamed my children would lose their mother I never dreamed I would lose my wife . . .

The next day after the funeral I sat alone in our house. Or was it my house now? The boys decided to go back to school and try to resume their lives. Motherless lives they now were. I cried big heavy tears on the couch. My girl was gone. I wondered where she was, floating somewhere, maybe talking to God, making Him a quilt. I'm sure God would have loved one of her quilts. Everywhere I looked I saw her. In the wallpaper, the furniture, the sponge-painted walls, all the many things she made for our beautiful home. Especially in the dining room is where I saw her. That room was all Ann.

She was everywhere, but nowhere. Not sitting next to me, anyway. That's where I wanted her: healthy, vibrant, her hair pulled back wearing something pretty, reaching for my hand telling me everything would be all right. Watching television and eating popcorn, peeking around the corner looking for little people who were suppose to be in bed, poking at the past, peering at the future.

I cried, I think, because I couldn't have that anymore. The conversations Ann and I had in life, about life; those days were gone for me now, vanished in the night, stolen away.

In Ann's Mother's Journal, it comes to page that talked about adolescent children. Ann simply writes, "You're not adolescent yet."

2003, Eric, Collin, and our friend, Dan, in Quincy Marketplace, Boston, the same place Ann and I had our first date.

29 | THE FINAL ANALYSIS: HEAL THE WOUND

Moving on doesn't mean letting go.

Defining moments in life always reveal something. Maybe it's an emotion you never thought you were capable of expressing or a limitation exposed. Or perhaps you found a gift that had been dormant until now. Your character: now that's a given to be revealed, good or bad. Some people run away from the fire, others run to it, some just admire the flames and do nothing at all.

I wrote the vast majority of this book seven to eight years after Ann died. I think I needed some smooth waters to sail my boat on. I penned my words in, of all places, my dining room on the same Nichols and Stone table Ann and I bought when we first got married. The same table she made things on and on which the four of us enjoyed many great meals together. As I wrote, things seem to fall into my lap, like phone calls from old friends at just the right time with more descriptive views of what happened. I found writings that Ann made years ago and I think she'd hoped they would find their way into print. It felt like all these years later Ann was still orchestrating things.

I was taught so much by Ann, my wife. That a mother's love never dies, that the things that matter most in life cannot be bought, they are made, that it truly is better to have loved and lost than never loved at all, that all we ever have is the moment we now live in, and that the greatest feeling anyone can have is the feeling of amazing joy in knowing at some point in time, however small or large, you made a difference in someone's life.

Eight months after Ann died, the boys and I returned to the Gulf coast of Florida on a trip she had arranged for us knowing she'd never get to go. I told her we would go. It was strange just having the three of us. I kept looking for her; I even waited for her to be ready so we all could go to dinner. She never came. I felt for her on the other side of the bed but I reached at empty space. I looked for her in all things pretty: the sunset, the moon, and the gentle waves approaching the beach. She was there I suppose, but it wasn't like those many times before when I could touch her and hold her in my arms.

This was our first attempt, the boys and me, at moving on without her. A big attempt it was, going back to the place where the four of us enjoyed many great days in the warm salty air. Now we were missing someone. She warned me it wouldn't be easy. And though I couldn't see her or feel her, I heard her voice and it soothed me and I heard her telling me things like *lather up the boys with sun screen, be careful swimming in the ocean, the undertow can be dangerous,* and *why aren't you wearing a hat?*

If only for a moment, it was like the four of us again. Just like it was before. Taking care of her men, big and small, holding hands along the beach letting the breeze and the sun warm our bodies. Reaching back, compressing this moment and capturing it forever.

Looking back, it is hard to believe where the time has gone. I don't hear her voice as often as I use to. Maybe I should listen more. I know she would be proud of her boys, though. They have grown into the men she'd hoped they'd be, captains of football teams, college students, explorers of new worlds but most of all, gentlemen. I know I had a hand in that, but so did Ann. I asked Collin once, that if his mother ever came down from heaven now, would she recognize him? He simply replied, "Of course she would, Dad, she was my mother."

You can't go around grief . . .
You march through it.

He's right, she would have.

We have all moved on, the boys and I, and all who loved Ann. It's what she wanted us to do and with her help, we have. You can't go around grief, the circle brings you back. You march through it. Through the storms, sometimes crying with your head slung low off your shoulders, aching from your heels to your ears, and ironically it's the pain that gets you through the pain. Living it, owning it, allowing it to take up residence in you for a while, pouring out your heart to the moon on some bench in the middle of the night, your agonizing screams cutting though the thin cold air.

It's the pain that gets you through the pain. You follow it. You feel it. It beats you down and builds you back up. It leaves you empty so you can be full again. Without this pain, you're lost and numb following a path that leads you back to the same bench and the same screams, slightly muted maybe, a different day, all else untouched.

Moving on doesn't mean letting go. She'll always be with me. I have relocated her now to an accepting part of my heart that comforts the memories and messages. She, more than anyone, has made me into the person I am today. I have just merged back into traffic, the wind at my back, a smile on my face, and joy back in my heart. I am no longer drifting like I was that serendipitous night in the Irish pub, the night she rescued me. I am whole again, on solid ground, aiming higher each day. I have Ann to thank for that. I feel lucky to have lived a good part of my life with her, and every time I look at my two handsome sons she comes back to me and reminds me of what we once had. That can never be taken away. That's forever.

In Eric and Collin, Ann lives on.

EPILOGUE

As I write these final words, it's snowing outside my window. Flakes no bigger than dandruff blow in the cold wind, reaching their destination after a long fall from a large cloud. Spring is beckoning in the distance, and if I know anything about nature, I know that these snowflakes won't stay here long and they will go back where they came from.

Many years have now passed since that dreadful day in June when my world came crumbling down. Every now and then I reflect back on the person I was before Ann's diagnosis. If I could go back and talk to that person and tell him a thing or two, I would. I would whisper in that person's ear such words as be more patient, be more thoughtful, be less self-centered, worry less, and understand that life happens and sometimes we don't always comprehend

The lure of bigger and better stuff only weighs you down, while the love that surrounds you lifts you to new heights.

how or why. I would also tell that person that everything happens for a reason and maybe we don't get to know what that reason is until someone else decides to tell us.

Mostly, I would want to tell that person that what he was chasing wasn't nearly as beautiful or as meaningful as what he had all along. The lure of bigger and better stuff only weighs you down while the love that surrounds you lifts you to new heights.

I know that can't happen. There is no time machine to take me back to that person. There is no rewind switch. What is done is done.

But marching forward, the person I am today has far more wisdom and character than the person I was before. This journey has taken me to classrooms I would never have seen and taught me things I would never have known. I did not choose for Ann to get cancer. I don't know why she did; I don't know how she did, either. But what I do know is that the lessons are not in the hardships, they are in choosing how to respond to them. I am not the first person to lose a spouse or a loved one. I certainly won't be the last, but what made my journey a little different was that I was able take this life-changing experience and turn it into an advantage. I learned first how to grieve, and then I learned all over again how to live. We are all faced with adversity in our lives, some more profound than others, but all these challenges we deal with are designed to teach us something, and when they don't, it's no one's fault but our own.

Comfort doesn't bring growth, stress does. Character is not born from a field of daises; it's born from the battlefields of life when you're pushed to your furthest limits over and over again. Yet you come back for more, stronger than before, ready to meet new challenges. After you grieve, choose to live again. It sounds easy; it's not, but it can be done.

One day, like the snowflake, I figure I'll go home again, too. And I suspect Ann will be waiting to tell me a few things, like *you turned out to be a better father than I thought you'd be, look around and see what you've been missing,* and *now, let's talk about that book you wrote.*

This book was Ann's idea. After countless searches, and pouring my frustrations out to her that I couldn't find any books that even remotely portrayed the pain and struggle we were going through, and none could I find that was written from the caregiver's point of view, the person, like me, left behind. In one of my weaker moments of self-pity, Ann, ever the pragmatic woman, simply said to me, "Write your own damn book."

And so I did. I couldn't argue with her. After all, she was dying.

This was an enormous task for me, but the thought of one person, or a million people, benefiting from this story and the lessons learned pushed me forward.

The final lesson is also the greatest gift and it is this: the challenges we all face every day can make us in the long run stronger or weaker, but the choice of the two is ultimately ours to make. We can choose misery or we can choose joy. We can choose self-pity or we can choose perseverance. We can choose to be inspired or we can choose to inspire others.

If we are fortunate enough to find joy again in our lives, we'll know it not by the smiles on our faces, but by the happiness in our hearts and the satisfaction in knowing we are survivors.

In learning how to die, we learn how to live.

At the end of her life, Ann gave back all she had left to give and took nothing with her but the love she had for us in her heart. She told me on one of those final days that she felt "blessed to have loved and been loved by so many wonderful people."

We were blessed too.

ABOUT THE AUTHOR

JOHN O'SHAUGHNESSY grew up in Massachusetts and graduated from the University of Massachusetts at Lowell in 1979. He has worked in sales and marketing for Sealy Incorporated since 1993 and now lives in the suburbs of Detroit. His youngest son, Collin, will soon enter his first year of college, while his oldest son, Eric, is finishing his third year at Michigan State University in Lansing. *The Greatest Gift* is John's first book and he believes it will help anyone who has suffered through loss. And when you think about it, who hasn't?